DONALD H. McKNEW, JR., M.D.
National Institute of Mental Health
Children's Hospital,
George Washington University School of Medicine

LEON CYTRYN, M.D.
National Institute of Mental Health
Children's Hospital,
George Washington University School of Medicine

HERBERT YAHRAES

Why *Isn't* Johnny Crying?

Coping with Depression in Children

With a Foreword by Reginald S. Lourie, M.D.

W·W·NORTON & COMPANY·NEW YORK·LONDON

THE TEXT OF THIS BOOK is composed in photocomposition Janson, with display type set in Caslon. Composition and manufacturing are by The Maple-Vail Book Manufacturing Group. Book design by Marjorie J. Flock.

Library of Congress Cataloging in Publication Data
McKnew, Jr., Donald H.
    Why *isn't* Johnny crying?
    Bibliography: p.
    Includes index.
    1. Depression in children.   I. Cytryn, Leon.
II. Yahraes, Herbert.   III. Title.
[DNLM: 1. Depression—In infancy and childhood.   WM
171 M479w]
RJ506.D4M34   1983   618.92'8527   82–22556

ISBN 0-393-01724-9

W. W. Norton & Company, Inc., 500 Fifth Avenue, New York, N.Y. 10110
W. W. Norton & Company Ltd., 37 Great Russell Street, London WC1B 3NU

2 3 4 5 6 7 8 9 0

*In loving memory of my mother and sister, 1944,
victims of man's inhumanity to man*

LEON CYTRYN

To Elizabeth and Gretchen

DONALD MCKNEW

Contents

Foreword

*F*ROM THE TIME OF recorded history, feelings of sadness and depression have been known to be part of the human condition. They range from mild to severe, from acute to chronic. They are easily shaken or immobilizing, even to the point where one has the feeling that life is not worthwhile. However, the fact that children experience these same phenomena has been almost kept out of sight. It has remained for Drs. Cytryn and McKnew to bring childhood depression "out of the closet" and, with this book, into public awareness. They not only have identified and classified the problems associated with depression in the young but have outlined approaches to help treat and relieve even hopeless feelings. In the case of many depressed adolescents, such approaches can be lifesaving.

When considering the nature of depression in the young, it is useful to begin with a picture of the developmental roots of these children's problems, starting with postnatal life, and taking into account current studies and clinical experience.

It is very difficult to see a baby under a year of age as anything but a sweet bundle of innocence. However, it is a member of the human race and as a part of its inheritance has a set of genes that we now know may predispose a given individual to depressive illness. Among other determinants are increasingly identifiable, individual differences among babies. Some are "executive infants" who can use what has been called "sending power" to "teach" caretakers to meet their needs. In contrast, some are low-energy babies—and perhaps easy prey to neglect—who may give up hope of ever being part of another person and become prone to depression. This basis for depression is known to result possibly in at least a dozen forms of psychosomatic syndromes in the first year of life, ranging from a failure to thrive to kwashiorkor (severe malnutrition), marasmus (emaciation), and malfunctioning of the body's systems.

We are now able to identify in some infants in the first months of life a number of constitutional disorders that can interfere with appropriate attachment and bonding, even when good care is available. For example, some babies develop disorders that interfere with their ability to calm themselves down when stimulated by internal or external stressful events. The infants who have difficulty in achieving homeostasis or a steady state appear to have an immature capacity to integrate stimuli with controls. This is remediable, but if the difficulty is not dealt with in helping ways, a preoccupation with dependency can persist for many years. At the same time in such a case, although dependency can continue to be a preoccupation, the child may doubt that his or her needs will be met. Only time and longitudinal studies will tell if these earliest bases for depression will, if uninterrupted, be determinants of later depression. Many psychoanalysts already think so from their analytic studies of depressed children and adults.

Let us look at another example of how the inborn, uncorrected integrative difficulties can lead to later depression. It is generally accepted that at birth there is no (or incomplete) connection between the basic senses. If the senses do not become organized appropriately, we know that a prime basis for learning and other disabilities may develop. We also know that such handicaps lead too often to a poor self-image. A continuing poor self-concept, especially if unrecognized and / or unremedied, is a well-known basis for depression, and leads to failures that reinforce poor self-confidence.

Still using deficits in integrative capacities (also known as synthetic functions) as a model of early depressive determinants, there are early and later problems that center on an imbalance between levels of impulses and anxiety, and the capacity to control them. Unmodified hyperactivity as one outcome of such an impulse imbalance has been found to result in underlying depression by the time an individual reaches school age. In the presence of anxiety, even in the first year of life, there are some infants whose thinking and acting can become disorganized. Such patterns of loss of control often end in feelings of helplessness and even hopelessness and, finally, depression. This is particularly true when the child's defenses—such as trying to make others feel helpless as a way of trying to avoid becoming depressed—are ineffective.

Unfortunately, unresolved needs can lead to poor or incomplete handling of later, expectable sources of anxiety. This is evident in babies whose "eight-month" separation anxiety persists, even into adult life. Unresolved concerns over such issues as losing significant people, even if pushed under the surface and out of awareness, can be triggered by difficulty in dealing with change or overcoming fears of death. One of the patterns that babies use after protesting when parents leave is to turn away, thereby "getting rid of" the parents. What the baby doesn't see doesn't exist. The baby thus appears to indicate "you didn't leave me, I leave you." If parents are upset by this, the baby has learned an important lesson. The same thinking is frequent in attempted and successful suicide—"how are others feeling about my leaving them." Such individuals carefully work their suicide notes.

When there are expectable, unresolved fears of bodily damage at the same time that primitive aggression is being tested (approximately two and a half to four years of age), one of the answers can be turning the aggression against oneself. This too is a pattern particularly seen in some adolescent suicide attempts—"I hurt you by hurting myself." The desperation in these situations can result from a teenager's trying to avoid the depression that comes from hostile impulses being frustrated by the immobilization of aggressive impulses brought to this stage from much earlier in development.

These are only a few examples of how early experiences can become the basis of depressive personality themes and reactions. One can point out many more—such as the effect on development of physical defects that hinder functioning but are out of sight of others, which often results in a depressive affect. This is often in direct contrast to a child's responses to physical defects that are visible, such as in congenital amputees.

From a historical perspective on the importance of the earliest years in establishing depressive pathways, it was only about thirty years ago that there was the general belief (held, for example, by Anna Freud) that there were no fundamental depressions in children. When John Bowlby's *Maternal Care and Mental Health* appeared and Rene Spitz's *Hospitalism* was made available, there was an impasse in professional opinion. It was when Spitz's movies showing infants with anaclitic depression became available that the tables turned. Forty-five of the then forty-eight states in the U.S. passed laws abolishing institutions for babies, unfortunately even the good ones. Then early child development research began to flower. However, even before this new era, there were isolated, annotated cases of depressed babies. Back in the late 1890s, a picture of a depressed infant appeared in a German "picture book" of pediatrics. However, it remained for James Robertson in the 1950s to show in dramatic form with the movie, *A Two Year Old Goes to the Hospital,* how limited hospital visiting patterns resulted in depressed patients. The changes that resulted were also brought about in part by Milton Shore's *Red Is the Color of Hurting.*

The present book is a highly important one. It makes available to all what Drs. Cytryn and McKnew have done in not only creating awareness of childhood depression and its treatment but pointing the way to prevention. Another "first" is that the authors look at depression of the young from the perspective of important, recent work done using the neurosciences approach to the organism's brain and body functioning in adult depressions. Even though these exciting insights into the change in neurohumors and neurochemistry are not directly applicable to the still-maturing young organism, the next steps include studying these processes during early development.

We probably will never be able to eliminate depression. However, as we learn more about the origins of this bane of the human spirit, we can help and even prevent its destructive effects on human functioning.

Reginald S. Lourie, M.D., Med.Sc.D.

Preface

SEVERAL YEARS AGO, one of the authors was consulted about the seven-and-a-half-year-old son of a Midwestern physician who for some years had been unable to attend school regularly or to make any friends. He had been seen by a number of mental health professionals and attended special schools without noticeable benefit. When the family gave us the history of the child's symptoms, and after the boy himself was interviewed, it was quite clear that he was suffering from an episodic manic disorder which had not previously been diagnosed. The failure to properly diagnose and treat the child wasn't due to a lack of community mental health facilities, nor to a lack of resolve or financial means on his parents' part. Rather, the difficulty seemed to stem from the professional community's inability to accept that such a young child may suffer from a serious mood disorder. The situation is made all the more striking when one finds out that many members of this child's family had had manic-depressive illnesses starting at various ages, and that the father was a manic-depressive patient who himself had had manic episodes when he was a youngster. Even though the father benefited from lithium treatment, the latter was never offered to the child. It was only after the father heard about our work that he brought the son to one of us for consultation. After his return home with our diagnosis and treatment recommendation, the child's therapist dismissed both as nonsense and so did the school authorities and other mental health professionals. Thus far the family remains unable to benefit from what they have learned about their son.

The above story is dramatic but by no means unique. The child whose interview you will read at length in chapter 1 spent three years being followed periodically at the National Institutes of Health before anybody in his home community would accept his diagnosis and institute proper treatment. Since proper treatment was instituted, this child has greatly benefited from it and leads a relatively normal life.

Although childhood depression and mood disorders in general are now better recognized in the medical community, we felt it important to write this book to disseminate such information as widely as possible. We would hope that children like the little boy first described won't have to wait some years to see a doctor many hundreds of miles away to get a diagnosis, and that such diagnosis won't be scoffed at in the years to come. If we aren't noticing that Johnny is crying in solitude or inside, we need to look more closely. We hope this book will be this closer look. If it can in some way help the many children with mood disorders, and their parents, we will feel exceedingly gratified.

During the years that we have studied the problems discussed in this book, we have been encouraged, helped, and guided by a number of farsighted colleagues. We would like to single out three of them for mention: Dr. Reginald Lourie, Dr. Joseph Noshpitz, and Dr. William E. Bunney, Jr. We would like to thank Dr. Virginia Mermel and Anna Williams for their help in editing and preparing the manuscript. We also want to acknowledge the generous support of our publisher, especially Norton editor Donald Fusting, without whose perseverance and support this task could not have been completed.

This book was written by the authors in their private capacities; no official support or endorsement from the Department of Health and Human Services is intended or should be inferred.

Donald H. McKnew, Jr.
Leon Cytryn
Herbert Yahraes

ONE

Introduction

It's a coming-and-going thing. I don't feel depressed all the time. Usually it takes something, no matter how minor, to really set it off, and I start feeling bad about something and I can't do anything, and so today everything's been going pretty well, so I don't feel bad at all. But on another day, you know, I might just not want to get up in the morning or do anything at all. . . . Just like everything's worthless, like it's just not worth it to even be. That's about the best I can do. It's—it seems like it's a silly thing to even go through life and exist. And from one day to the next you're always wondering if you're going to make it to the next day if it's—if you can stand it, if it's worth trying to get to tomorrow. . . . It's just—just, I feel like—I feel mostly like I'm worthless, like there's something wrong with me. It's really not a pleasant feeling to know that you're a total failure, a complete nothing, and I get the feeling that I didn't do nothing right or worthwhile or anything.

DEPRESSION IN ADULTS is a sad, lonely, and at times tragic experience. In children it can be even more devastating, as illustrated by these observations made by a teen-age boy.

As a young professor of pediatrics, one of the authors, Leon Cytryn, was struck by the frequency of sadness and withdrawal in preadolescent and early adolescent boys who were admitted to a pediatric hospital for a surgical repair of undescended testicles (cryptorchism). This observation led to a research project to explore specifically the emotional adjustment of children with this condition. The results of the study indicated that of the boys with undescended testicles, especially those in whom the surgical repair was delayed beyond the age of eight years, almost half were seriously emotionally disturbed. Of those, most had symptoms closely associated with adult depression, such as sad mood, poor self-esteem, social withdrawal, poor school performance, and a feeling of hopelessness.

Intrigued by these findings, Cytryn collaborated in studies exploring the emotional adjustment of children with four types of chronic illness: cystic fibrosis, congenital heart disease, sickle-cell anemia, and congenital amputation. In each of these illnesses but congenital amputation, the findings were similar to those in the previous study of boys with undescended testicles. Close to half of the children showed symptoms of emotional disturbance characterized by depressive symptoms (sadness, withdrawal, impairment in functioning, social isolation, helplessness, and hopelessness) and/or symptoms of anxiety (separation anxiety, fear of strangers, phobic avoidance, tension, irritability, and sleep disturbances).

Several years later Cytryn, a pediatric psychiatrist, returned to a large pediatric university hospital where his duties included making teaching rounds biweekly on the pediatric and surgical wards, accompanied by medical students, interns, and residents. The children seen by Cytryn suffered either from a medical or a surgical illness. None had been diagnosed as having an emotional disorder.

Yet many of these physically ill children appeared to be markedly depressed, according to all the criteria used at that time to diagnose adult depression. Puzzled, Cytryn wondered if they did not in fact suffer from the same condition that afflicted depressed adults or, at least, from a related condition. Furthermore, he wondered whether such a depressive condition might exist in children who do not have a concomitant physical illness or handicap and who have never been hospitalized.

At the time, Donald McKnew was also working with hospitalized children, in a large hospital in another city. Here the children were not physically ill or injured; rather, they were in a mental hospital, having been admitted for a variety of reasons. Two diagnoses predominated. One was schizophrenia, the name given to a group of psychotic disorders marked by disturbances of thought, behavior, and mood. The other principal diagnosis was conduct disorder, wherein patients use a variety of antisocial behaviors to express their emotional conflicts.

Like Cytryn, McKnew was impressed by his observation that a number of the children he encountered were extremely sad, withdrawn, and lethargic most of the time and expressed feelings of low self-esteem, hopelessness, and despair. He wondered whether these children might not suffer from depression, either as their main illness, or secondary to their presenting illness, or simply because they were in a hospital. Both McKnew and Cytryn were aware that a diagnosis of childhood depression was not acceptable to the medical profession in those days; medical teaching insisted that children did not become depressed in a clinical sense. It occurred to McKnew to question whether the children who seemed depressed had blood abnormalities similar to those reported in depressed adults. He attempted to elicit the cooperation of the endocrinology department in order to study some of the biochemical abnormalities known to exist in depressed adults. Unfortunately no one was willing to cooperate, since the notion seemed preposterous.

Soon afterward, McKnew accepted a staff appointment at Children's Hospital in Washington, D.C., where he met Cytryn. The two discussed their experiences with childhood depression and almost immediately began to collaborate in studying the subject. That collaboration has lasted fifteen years and still continues. Gradually, other child psychiatrists and members of other medical specialties have become interested, and today childhood depression is a widely recognized condition. There are official guidelines for diagnosing it and a variety of drugs for use along with psychotherapy in treating it.

Adult Depression: An Ancient Malady

Depression is certainly the most widespread mental and emotional disorder afflicting mankind, and very probably the oldest. In ancient days it harassed Job, that wealthy, God-fearing Old Testament character who—at the instigation of Satan—is suddenly stricken by a succession of calamities. Enemies kill his herdsmen and drive off his cattle; fire from the skies burns up his thousands of sheep and his shepherds; marauders kill his camel drivers and drive off the camels; a whirlwind strikes the home of one of his sons and kills all ten of Job's children. Satan had predicted that when Job had thus been ruined he would curse the Lord. But Job says only, "The Lord gave, and the Lord hath taken away; blessed be the name of the Lord." Then Satan, having received the Lord's permission to strike at the man himself, afflicts Job with sores from head to foot. At this point Job's wife advises him to "curse God and die." Job answers, "Shall we receive good at the hand of God, and shall we not receive evil?" To friends who argue that he is being punished for his sins, he declares his innocence. Society despises him. Finally, he is driven to deny that God is just. Distraught and deeply depressed, he longs for death. As the story so vividly portrays, Job over a long period of time wards off feelings of despair over his numerous afflictions. However, he finally succumbs and displays symptoms of what we would now label a reactive depression. Undoubtedly, depression has afflicted people for many thousands of years. It was the only recognized mental illness in antiquity and its description in the writings of Hippocrates and Galen, the leading physicians of ancient Greece and Rome, respectively, rivals any modern description in clarity and perceptiveness. Today it is found in all countries and cultures. In one way or another it has affected Abraham Lincoln, Winston Churchill, Theodore Roosevelt, Honoré de Balzac, Vincent van Gogh, Ernest Hemingway, and many others. In the United States alone it afflicts millions of people.

Despite its ancient history and universal range, depression in its various forms has until recently remained a mysterious malady whose causes could only be guessed at and whose treatment was largely guesswork. During the last twenty years, however, medical scientists have begun to answer many important questions surrounding it. Of most importance for the time being, they have learned in the great majority of cases to treat it effectively. During this same period, child psychiatrists have discovered that children are common victims of depression as well. To parents, teachers, physicians, counselors, and all other persons concerned with the welfare of the family, this is a finding of tremendous importance, because a depressed child usually goes undiagnosed or misdiagnosed. Often he or she is considered to have simply a behavior problem. Though childhood depression is harder than adult depression to diagnose, it can be treated just as effectively. And there are indications that if treatment begins early the disease may not progress into adulthood.

A Depressed Boy Tells His Story

The following is a slight condensation of an interview
conducted by one of us not long ago with a boy of high-
school age who had a major depressive disorder.* The
questions, put by Dr. McKnew, are answered directly by
the boy, who comes from a middle-class family.

What does your depression feel like today?

It's a coming-and-going thing. I don't feel depressed all
the time. Usually it takes something, no matter how minor,
to really set it off, and I start feeling bad about something
and I can't do anything, and so today everything's been
going pretty well, so I don't feel bad at all. But on another
day, you know, I might just not want to get up in the morning or do anything at all.

Can you tell me more about it? What else do you feel?

Just like everything's worthless, like it's just not worth
it to even be. That's about the best I can do. It's—it seems
like it's a silly thing to even go through life and exist. And
from one day to the next you're always wondering if you're
going to make it to the next day if it's—if you can stand it,
if it's worth trying to get to tomorrow. And—

Can you tell me what the hurt feels like a little bit?

Ah—not really. It's just—just, I feel like—I feel mostly
like I'm worthless, like there's something wrong with me.
It's really not a pleasant feeling to know that you're a total
failure, a complete nothing, and I get the feeling that I didn't
do nothing right or worthwhile or anything. Just—

Does it make you feel hopeless about life?

Yes. That's a very good way to describe it . . .

---

*© American Broadcasting Companies, Inc. 1981. Reprinted by permission
of ABC News.

Off and on, how long have you had some of these feelings? Can you date it back?

. . . I really started having problems like with school and things when I was in—well, that was about two years ago. Then before that, I really was hating school and missed, was absent, an awful lot. But I was always able to return and get back into things. And my grades really started to slip, and before that, I just plain old didn't like school. I had trouble making myself go all the time. But I've always done really well in school. It's not a matter of having trouble with getting the grades or anything like that. It was just a matter of hating it, getting up in the morning—

No pleasure?

That's probably the worst. Yeah. And I never really got along with other people at school that well—at least not since elementary school. So I'd have to say it started about sixth grade or, you know, maybe five, six years ago that I really started getting down . . .

Even before that?

Yeah. Just—well, I've always—everyone tells me, anyway, that I've been a perfectionist. I don't even know exactly what that means, but I know that I was never doing things well enough to suit myself since—well, ever since I can remember. It's—nothing's ever been quite good enough. And then it kind of snowballed, and I got—it got so nothing was even good. And then everything was bad that I did, and then everything's terrible, and—

Yeah. And these last two years with school, sort of was—it progressed? To just not being able to go at all?

Yeah. I just—I got to hating school so much and hating my life in general. I was really getting to be a bore, and didn't like it, and one morning the alarm went off and I was lying there in bed and saying, "I have to get up to go to school . . . but I—I can't. I don't know what I'm going to do. I just can't get up." I couldn't do it. I couldn't make myself get up and get ready for school. No matter what—I just sat there and thought to myself, "What am I going to do?"—you know, and my whole life flashed before my eyes, and, you know, everything's going wrong and it felt like the end of the world, that I just couldn't do anything.

And then that continued on for days, and my mother would come in and say, you know—"Are you getting up for school today?" And I wouldn't say anything, because I didn't want to say, "No, I don't want to go to school," because it wasn't true. I wanted to be able to go to school and just go and get it over with, but I couldn't say, "Yes, I'm going," 'cause I knew I wasn't deep down inside. I knew there was no way I was going to school that day.

When you've really gotten as down as you can get, you've told me in the past you've thought about hurting yourself. Could you describe some of that?

I'm really afraid of pain, so it's not so much a matter of hurting myself. I just wish I wasn't what I was at all. I wish I wasn't alive. I wish there was some way I could just disappear off the face of the earth, never have been born or something along that line. If you're asking me did suicide come up, yeah, a lot. That was in my mind an awful lot. But I—

But you hate pain—

Yeah, that's right. Well, let's see—the best way I could think of was a drug overdose or something like that. That was all I could really think of, because—well, I couldn't blow my brains out—I didn't have a pistol or anything like that. That was for sure. And besides, that would hurt. There wasn't really much to it. I just—I'd think, "Boy, I wish I was dead," and then I'd think, "That's ridiculous," you know, " 'cause you're never going to be able to kill yourself. You don't have enough guts for that."

You're a flop at suicide too.

Yeah. Right. That entered my mind—

Good Lord. Isn't that something. Now there've been a lot of efforts to try to do something to make it better for you. You came to see me a little over a year ago. What seems to get in the way of getting some help for you?

Well, children—well, I guess I should say adolescents— aren't real people at all in this world. You know, they don't have real, live emotions or feelings. They can't think; they can't do; they're possessions and they kind of exist. And so no one has really even thought about, you know, what's wrong with the kid. You know, it's just—it was a matter of, well, he'll either "grow out of it" or something like this. You know, "If we just talk to him for a while," you know. "It's obvious that he's just not being logical about anything." Which was—couldn't be further from the truth.

You mean your feelings weren't taken seriously?

Yeah.

What you felt was a bunch of baloney 'cause you're just a kid and can't feel—

Yeah. I was just being dumb or trying to get attention or something like that, you know. So I went to a few counselors and things, and they told me that, you know, that I would just have to set goals in my life and, you know, that I would have to want to go to school. . . . Like—well, "Next week, what you're going to have to do is, say, you're going to have to make up your mind to go to school and then go and just do it." Or I'd get a lot of advice like, "You don't have to be an all-A student or anything. Just get through it. Just go, do the least amount you can do, and—" But that's impossible—at least for me . . .

Yeah. And what happened to the idea of trying to get some medicine that might make you—?

Ah, yeah. I finally got on an antidepressant from my

family doctor, who I guess would probably be one of the wisest people I've ever met. He's really, really nice and smart, and I liked him a lot. . . . When I finally went back to a psychiatrist, he said that—he told my Mom that it was— that it was okay if I wanted to get off of it, to discontinue it. And which I did, because I felt kind of bad about being dependent on this stuff to be able to get up in the morning and to function.

Although it was helping you.

Yeah. I—it must have, because I was able to go back to school, at least temporarily. But it had side effects and stuff, and I didn't like it, so I decided to get off of it. I was going to, and the psychiatrist told my Mom that it was okay that I should get off. So I got off and got really depressed and quit school again, and it all went back to the way—way it was before.

If you could tell us what a day in your life feels like right now—I know we've talked about it, but if you could do it again it would be very helpful.

Well, okay. It would—I—first of all, I'd stay up really late worrying about the next day. Okay. And that would turn into the day. It would go past one or two, 'cause when I get depressed, I don't sleep at all. And I'd really start worrying about the next day—I'm—and what I'm going to do when my mother comes in and asks me whether I'm going to school or not, and, you know, what's going to happen when I don't do anything. So it comes time in the morning, and my Mom comes in and gets me up, and asks me if I'm going to school, and I don't say anything. I just bury myself as far into the pillows as I can, and she leaves, being rather upset and miserable about the whole thing. Okay.

So I lay in bed, and if I can go back to sleep, great,

'cause then that's kind of an escape for, what, another two hours? I don't have to exist [*laughs*]. I don't have to worry about anything or anything like that. So—but if I can't, then I just start thinking about how lousy everything is going for me. Here I am laying in bed doing absolutely nothing all day. I'm not a—I'm not a sitter. I don't sit back and watch things happen. I—I—I do all right. I go after things that I want—usually. But this depression just absolutely incapacitates me. I can't do anything. I can't do anything I want to do; I can't do anything I don't want to do. I can't make myself do anything . . . I don't even get up to eat. The only time I can eat is when everyone's gone to bed, because then I don't have to look 'em in the face or see 'em at all. 'Cause I feel really bad about not having done what I was supposed to do for that day, you know. Especially as a child, there are certain things you're expected to do day in and day out, each day. You're supposed to go to school, you're not supposed to skip classes or anything—blah, blah, blah, blah, etcetera [*sighing*]. And—and I don't do any of these things that I'm supposed to do—at all—when I get depressed. And that makes it worse, 'cause I feel bad about not doing the things I was supposed to do.

And tell me again a little bit about the pain that this then makes you feel.

Well, I suppose most people don't have something— well, I don't know—this—it's something that you hate so intensely that you have to do day in and day out, and I'm not talking about going to school, either. I'm talking about being, living with me. I just hate it so much. I just don't like what I am and who I am and what I stand for and what I do. Just hate it so intensely that, well, if you can't forget it, you just have to try to push it out of your mind, 'cause it—it'll tear you right up. There's nothing you can do—just sit there and mumble to yourself over and over again, "Oh, I hatè myself, and," you know, "I hate you," talking to yourself . . .

And do you feel sort of empty and—and devoid of any sense of purpose or—?

Well, not an empty kind of feeling, but just like you're full, you're full of nothing. I've—you've—you've got this fantastic ability to do wrong and bad, and stuff—

Oh. So you're full of bad feelings rather than just devoid of—

Yeah. And you feel really alone because no one understands—at all. Totally—you know. I even talked to kids my age, and they say, "Yeah, I know how you feel. I really hate school too." But if they did [*laughing*] they wouldn't go. I—I found that out pretty quickly. If you hate something that bad . . .

You take any pleasure in—in anything?

Yeah. I like music a lot—I played in the band and sang in choir at school—and theater and the people. I like people a lot. I like being around 'em as much as possible . . .

When you do those things, do you come up a little bit, and—

Yeah. You forget. If you get busy enough, you forget what's going on. You forget that you don't feel bad—it sounds kind of silly, but you think if you could forget that you don't feel bad, then you don't, but you—you still do. You feel terrible. And then if something goes wrong while you're doing something fun, like you make a mistake or something, oh, you just—you feel like "Well, that's it. I'm—even at something I enjoy doing, I'm no good." You just kind of feel like giving up . . .

[*To the boy's mother*] *I was wondering if you might share with us some of how you viewed your son's adventures through the land of depression.*

[Mother] Well, it was a very difficult—I didn't realize he was having problems with depression at a young age.

He—the school thing was like he did very well at the beginning, and then it—it would drop off as it went along. But two years ago, he had a viral infection, and they thought it was mononucleosis. And I took him to a doctor, and he was sure it was, so he told me to keep him out of school, because this is a long kind of disease, and so I did. . . . By the time we found that it wasn't mono, he had missed like a semester of school. He kept saying he was so depressed at this time, during the time when he—we thought he had mono.

And I read books and stuff, and it says that viral infections sometimes will bring on a depression. So I went to my family doctor, and I told him that my son was very depressed. And he said—this is not the same family doctor we'd been to talk with before—he said, "What's he got to be depressed about? You know, after all, he's just a kid. Why should he be depressed?"

———————

These last sentences show how many of us felt and acted when confronted with cases of childhood depression, and still too often do: "After all, he's just a kid. Why should he be depressed?" As we go along, we'll discuss many reasons why even "just a kid" becomes depressed.

Cases like the foregoing one go unrecognized year after year. They continue to go unrecognized even as more is known about childhood depression. It is a tragedy.

Depression among Children

Because of our personal experiences, we have been interested in all aspects of childhood depression: its etiology, recognition, treatment, and prevention. We have studied and treated children from all social classes. No matter what the family environment was like, the basic symptoms of depression were the same from child to child.

Recently we have been studying a group of thirty children each of whom has a close relative who has been hospitalized for treatment of a major depressive illness. One girl, a worried-looking ten-year-old, told us: "I am the biggest trouble-maker in our family. I cry a lot and feel weird a lot." Speaking in a tense, slow voice—a monotone—she added that she doesn't sleep well, feels ugly, and has thought of suicide. She joked about jumping out of the window. Then she mentioned some dreams she's had. In one of them she leaves the house and, when she tries to return, cannot find it. In another she runs away and injures her foot.

A twelve-year-old boy was sad, tense, and fidgety. In a low voice, and between spells of crying, he told us that he feels sad, lonely, and inferior. "I think I am the stupidest kid in class," he said. "I never really try to kill myself, but sometimes I think to drown myself." He drew a plane and said: "It will kill people on the beach."

A girl of eleven was relaxed, showed only occasional signs of sadness, and spoke softly. She stays alone much of the time, she said, and cries sometimes when criticized. She told about her dreams. In one series she is in a maze and dogs are chasing her; she is caught by a man with a gun, hurts her leg, and can't get up. In another series, a girl dies, a boy runs away from his stepfather, and King Arthur's kingdom is destroyed.

Although none of the thirty studied who has a depressed close relative was psychotic or insane, all scored higher than average on tests for depressive symptoms in young people. The children were as young as four and as old as fifteen. More than 50 percent of them, it turned out, clearly were depressed.

Among children in the United States, the percentage who have clear symptoms of depression is much lower (though still much higher than anyone imagined half a dozen years ago). Our studies, some of which will be discussed later, indicate that it ranges from 5 percent to 10 percent. This finding for children is close to the estimated proportion of adults who are affected—about 10 percent. On the basis of these findings, *from three to more than six million American children suffer from depression—much of it unrecognized and untreated.* The figure for adults runs to fifteen million or more.

The Nicest Kid on the Block

Why has depression in children gone unrecognized all this time? For thousands of years adults have been known to be afflicted by it; for thousands of years physicians and others have written about its occurrence in adults. Yet its presence in children was missed until a dozen or so years ago. From our experience, perhaps the biggest reason is that many depressed children are often the "nicest" boys and girls on the block and the best behaved kids in school. Go into a classroom and you'll find that the kids in the back rows are the quiet ones, the ones that don't give anyone any trouble, though we know now that many of them are depressed. They're usually well mannered and often shy, and they seem to like to help people. The mischief-makers, the hyperactive children, the kids with behavior disorders—they're up front where the teacher can easily keep an eye on them. A parallel situation exists on most pediatric wards, where the depressed children are usually found tucked away in the corner far from the nurses' desk. The nurses are unaware of the difficulty because of the children's "nice" behavior and the fact that they give nobody any trouble.

As a matter of fact, many depressed adults are like these well-behaved children. Some of them are the nicest people, the most thoughtful, the hardest working. Maybe it sounds odd, but often the thing a psychiatrist has to do is to get them to look out for their own needs and welfare and not go on trying to take care of everybody else.

Unless you know a depressed child quite well and are really looking for signs of depression, you probably won't notice anything wrong. But if you ask him, "How are you really feeling today?" he'll probably answer, "I feel awful"; or, as the adolescent said in the previous interview, "You just kind of feel like giving up . . ."

What makes many depressed children and adults seem uncomplaining and so eager to help others? We suspect that an important part of the answer to this question lies in a poor self-image and a deep-seated conflict over the handling of hostile and angry feelings. The fear that angry feelings may be potentially harmful to oneself or to others may teach a depressed person to avoid or even suppress such feelings at any cost. Unfortunately, the price exacted by this process may be extremely high in terms of personal suffering. In the beginning of this chapter, in describing Leon Cytryn's findings of depressive symptoms in children with chronic illness and handicaps, we alluded to the fact that children with congenital amputation have been surprisingly free of emotional disturbance. This finding has been confirmed by researchers in Canada, England, and Germany. When we investigated this phenomenon, we discovered that these children shared a remarkable freedom, fostered by their parents and caretakers, to express their aggression openly. Such an externalization of aggression seemed to have been a protection against the development of depressive symptoms seen in most severely handicapped children. This crucial relationship between depression and aggression will be elaborated in subsequent chapters.

A preliminary finding from a study we are presently

engaged in indicates that even among one-year-olds who appear to be depressed, many are terrified of any hostility and try to ward it off or end it by acting as caretakers to their own parents. These babies actually seem to be going out of their way to be nice to their mothers and to cause no trouble. It could be that such children are often the forerunners of the quiet, shy, caretaking, depressed person that we see later on in childhood, in adolescence, and in adulthood.

TWO

What Is Childhood Depression?

*D*EPRESSION IS A STATE that is common to all mankind and to many animals. It is marked by sadness, a feeling of worthlessness, and a conviction that nothing one can do matters. Under many circumstances, depression may be quite appropriate—for example, when a loved one dies or when you suffer other loses, real or imagined. If a friend leaves town, if you move to another neighborhood, if your children have to change schools—all these and many other circumstances may give you the blues and make you feel low and depressed for days and even weeks. Each of us experiences this type of depression at one time or another. We are not clinically depressed but in a depressed mood.

However, there is a point at which such a response to loss and other sources of stress stops being appropriate and becomes a type of mental illness. This book will be devoted in large part to how we know when a child is nearing the danger point, how we can prevent him or her from reaching it, and how we can restore to health a child with a depressive disorder.

Differences between Mood or Affect and Disorder

Parents often ask how to distinguish between a depressed mood or affect and a depressive disorder. (Mood and affect are synonymous.) One way is to notice the duration and intensity of the condition. A child who shows no signs of being comforted or of resuming a normal life within a week after falling into a low mood (for whatever reason)—or within six months after undergoing what is to him a severe loss—is at risk of developing a depressive disorder.

Another measure is the ability of the stricken child to function in everyday life. Does the child play as much as usual? Keep up with his or her class in school? Perform work adequately? Engage in the usual activities? If the answer is still No a week after the depressed behavior sets in, the child is reaching the point where he or she is at risk of experiencing more serious consequences.

Sudden changes in eating and sleeping patterns can be an indicator, too. Appetite often either falls off or increases with the start of a depressive disorder. If it doesn't return to normal within a few weeks, the child needs help. The same is true of sleep problems. Among these are failure to fall asleep at the usual time; waking up during the night and having trouble getting back to sleep; and waking up in the morning unusually early. A depressed child may get a great deal of sleep and still feel constantly tired.

In some extreme cases, the presence of suicidal tendencies is a giveaway. Some depressed children have suicidal thoughts. As their depression deepens, they may plan and even attempt suicide. Usually they keep the thoughts to themselves, but gentle probing can bring them out. Fifty percent of all depressed children, if they are asked, will talk about thoughts of at least hurting themselves.

Most of us have heard or read a good deal about depressive disorders in adults and very little or nothing about such illness in children. Many of us know adults who are depressed. Children do not show their depression so openly—do not wear it on their sleeve, as adults do. Children tend to be depressed in an extremely quiet way. They go to their rooms, out to the barn, go off quietly and cry while tending to appear cheerful in public settings. Furthermore, they don't look as sad, tearful, or slowed down as depressed adults. By the time a child exhibits signs of depression for all to see, he or she usually is severely depressed. The level of depression that is obvious in an adult often goes unrecognized in children by teachers, parents, and even friends.

For some of us, a more powerful reason than the above for the difference in visibility between childhood and adult depression is the way we view childhood. Looking back on it, we tend to view childhood as a happy time, though many children do not look on it that way, and though Charles Dickens and other perceptive novelists certainly have not. Recalling our own childhood through the rainbow-colored mists of time, many of us see the early years as a period during which a child could not possibly be depressed, except momentarily.

Depression in Adults

Beyond the bouts of temporary depressive moods that most of us experience at one time or another and usually pull through on our own, there are two serious types of adult depression. Medicine and, often, psychotherapy are needed to treat either one. The two are known as *unipolar* and *bipolar*. If these names are unfamiliar, think of a pole with one end marked *depression* and the other end *mania*. The unipolar patient is at the depressive end of the pole.

The bipolar patient travels from one end to another.

An adult with the unipolar type of depression is obviously down for a significant period of time. No matter how hard he tries, he cannot find happiness either in work or in recreation. He is acutely dispirited. A former patient has written that he lived "in a world in which the sun had gone down and never come up again, in which fear was the dominant emotion, a world in which there was no joy." Many times the unipolar adult is listless, finds it very hard or even impossible to go about his work and other customary activities, and may think about—or bring himself to commit—suicide. Sometimes, however, unipolar illness may simply drag a person into a state of the blues without seriously interfering with work. It will probably interfere more with his social life, both because he lacks energy and because he is not a companionable person to be around.

The adult with bipolar illness is sad and dispirited when he reaches the depressed end of the pole, agitated and excited when he reaches the manic end. Such a person is often referred to as *manic-depressive*. During the manic period he may feel unusually well and strong, may go without sleep for long periods, and, because he feels like Superman, may plunge into vast, foolish undertakings in his personal or business affairs. Psychiatrist Nathan Kline, an authority on depressive disorders, tells about a man from a very wealthy family who had been treated for depression and suddenly became manic, telephoned his brokers, and placed orders for almost half a million dollars worth of stocks.* Kline tells also of a woman patient who went into a department store to buy some dish towels and ended up spending six thousand dollars. At the opposite or depressive pole, says Kline, "aggressive action is replaced by extreme withdrawal,

* Kline, 1974.

chronic excitement gives way to listless torpor, and in extreme cases the patient becomes unable to manage the simplest matters." He may attempt suicide. As a rule, bipolar adults are more seriously ill than unipolor. Unipolar and bipolar illness are thought to be hereditary, usually cause some degree of incapacitation, and sometimes occur in a psychotic form. The majority of adults with mood disorders, however, have a milder form of depression, called *minor, dysthymic,* or *neurotic depression.* This disorder is generally characterized by less impairment, fewer symptoms, absence of psychosis, and a shorter time course. For instance, the latest research indicates that a major depressive episode may last, on an average, two years, while the average duration of a minor depression is only six to nine months. While the biological and genetic basis of major affective illness is generally accepted, the same issue in minor depression is far from being settled.

Some Early Reports of Childhood Depression

While childhood depression has been recognized as a separate disorder for about fifteen years only, it is of interest that depressive states in infants and young toddlers have been described in great detail by several child psychoanalysts over the past seventy years.

One such person was a psychiatrist named Rene Spitz. He had been interested in child development when in the 1940s he came upon 123 young children being raised in a South American nursery. He found that a number of them tended to withdraw from social contact, lose weight, have trouble sleeping, and become ill—behavior much like that being noticed by doctors nowadays in many older children who have suffered a loss and become depressed. Spitz called this behavior *anaclitic* (leaning upon) *depression.* It lasted up to three months, after which some patients assumed a rigid, frozen posture.

Spitz searched for a common cause of such behavior. He found that all the children who developed the symptoms cited above had been separated from their mothers somewhere between the sixth and eighth month of life for an unbroken period of at least three months. They had had no mother or good mother-substitute to lean upon, hence the term "anaclitic." When the separation ended in less than six months, Spitz found, usually the children suddenly turned "friendly, gay, approachable, and the withdrawal, disinterest, and rejection of the outside world, the sadness disappeared as if by magic."*

How about the children whose mothers did not come back and who lacked a good substitute? Spitz was able to study that question in a foundling home, where the lost mothers had not been restored. Here the picture of depression was as clear-cut as in the nursery but continued to a more advanced stage. In the worst cases, the children became either stuporous, agitated, or retarded. It appeared that most could not be brought back to normal. In fact, twenty-four of the ninty-one who were studied died as a result of their condition.

One of the first child psychiatrists, an Englishman named John Bowlby, in the 1950's began studying the relationship between child and mother and stressed what most of us now know. The child is dependent on the mother not only physically—for food, clothing, warmth, cleanliness, and transportation—but also emotionally—that is, for love, tenderness, empathy, closeness to another human being. This emotional dependence is so strong that child development authorities often speak of it as a bond or attachment.

*Spitz, 1945, 1946.

When the mother disappears for even a short while, the baby may cry, search for her with his eyes, or, if he is in the crawling or toddling stage, try actively to find her.

When mother and child were separated for a long time or forever, Bowlby found, the baby's reaction can be separated into three distinct stages. At first he seems acutely distressed. He cries, yells, and appears to be trying—for instance, by looking everywhere he knows—to get the mother back. Bowlby calls this stage *protest*. It lasts from a few hours to a few weeks. Next came a stage that Bowlby calls *despair*. The child seems to have lost all hope. He looks depressed. He withdraws from his usual activities and is apathetic. Finally, Bowlby noticed a stage he called *detachment*, in which the child seems to have accepted the help given by nurses and other mother-substitutes. However, when the child has lost not only his mother but a series of mother-substitutes, he gradually loses trust in all human beings and shows an attitude of indifference to human contact. Later, in the 1960s, Margaret S. Mahler, one of the foremost child psychoanalysts, agreed with Bowlby's observation that children's depressed moods can be caused predominantly by separation. Like Bowlby, she believes that these moods create a basis for depressive states later in life.

Probably Mahler's best-known work is her close study of the way normal children ordinarily separate from their mothers and become individuals. She closely observed the interaction between young mothers and their youngest children in a day nursery in New York. The mothers talked to one another or read, and cared for their children as usual. The children played or slept. The study began when the children were about five months old and continued through their third year. This is the period during which the child usually completes the process of breaking away from the mother, the so-called *separation-individuation process*.

Mahler and her associates talk about two sisters, A and Susan, as good examples of the mother's special importance during the period when the child is becoming an individual. Toward the end of the first year of life, when children are beginning to realize that there is more to the world than themselves and their mothers, Ann often sat at her mother's feet and patiently begged for attention. Most often she begged in vain. The investigators say that, as a result, she had little psychic energy for the next period of her development, the *practicing phase*. During this period, Mahler found, the normal child takes delight in trying out his new skills, particularly his ability to get around by himself. He crawls or walks further and further from his mother's feet and often becomes so absorbed in his activities that for long periods of time he seems oblivious to his mother's presence. But Ann would make only brief excursions away from her mother. This period in which the usual child is exuberant lasted only a relatively short while for her, and she acted subdued during most of it.

Later, Ann was plainly an unhappy little girl who could not easily endure separation from her mother, did not get along well with other adults and children, and showed little joy when her mother returned after short, everyday absences. In one camera-recorded scene she has a tantrum when her mother starts to leave the room. At first she insists on going along but then gives up and just stands there, suffering. Finally, she regresses by retiring to the play area for the youngest babies. She turns her back on the others and is clearly hurt and angry.

Ann is described as already vulnerable—already in trouble. Unless through further experience the girl is amply compensated for the rejections and other disappointments of her earliest years, the investigators believe she may well develop emotional problems.

Ann's younger sister, Susan, entered the ⌐er was still somewhat aloof and self-cen-⌐d mellowed. Every so often she would put ⌐ and bury herself in the newspaper. But ⌐outward-going and determined than Ann. When she wanted her mother's attention, she knew how to go about getting it. In one photographed scene, she tugs at her mother's dress, looks beseechingly at her, and finally starts to pull herself up to her mother's knee. The viewer can almost hear the mother say, "Oh, the heck with it," as she lays down the paper and lovingly picks up the baby. Some time later, Susan looks distressed when her mother leaves the room, but—unlike Ann—soon turns happily to playing with others in the room. She is joyful when her mother returns. Mahler emphasizes that a child who has a good relationship with her mother shows relatively little tendency toward depression and is better prepared emotionally than other children to handle what life offers.

These early reports by Bowlby, Spitz, and Mahler have one thing in common: they're impressionistic. Their subjects were raised under unusual circumstances. Often they come from nurseries and orphanages and broken homes. These pioneers (with the possible exception of Mahler) did not link the depressive states in infancy and early childhood to depression in later life. Nevertheless, their contributions are invaluable, both conceptually and historically.

Classification of Depression in Children

Childhood depression has been generally recognized as a distinct illness for little more than a dozen years. Before that, as pointed out in chapter 1, it had been usually ignored or else treated as a behavior disorder. One of the first to classify it was Warren A. Weinberg, who, with colleagues at Washington University in St. Louis, drew up a set of criteria in the early 1970s.

These criteria or benchmarks for depression were that the child show both an unhappy mood and a sense of self-depreciation, and two or more of the following symptoms: aggressive behavior, sleep disturbance, lessened desire to socialize with people, change in attitude toward school, change in school performance, physical complaints, loss of usual energy, and unusual change in appetite or weight or both. The symptoms had to be different from the child's usual behavior, and they had to continue for at least one month.

Weinberg and his colleagues used their scheme to study seventy-two children, from six to twelve years old, who had been sent to a diagnostic center because they had been having trouble in school. Forty-two children—or 58 percent—met the criteria for depression.

About ten years ago we proposed a classification that described three types of depression in school-age children, or children from six to twelve. Under our classification, childhood depression was divided among three main types—acute, chronic, and masked.

The acute and chronic types have similar features. These include severe impairment of the child's scholastic and social adjustment; disturbances of sleep and eating; feelings of despair, helplessness, and hopelessness; retardation of movement; and occasional suicidal thoughts or attempts. The main difference between these two types lies in precipitating causes, the child's adjustment before illness, the length of the illness, and the family history. Children with chronic depression, in contrast to those with the acute type, have no immediate precipitating cause, their illness lasts longer, and there is a history of marginal social and emotional adjustment, of previous depressive episodes, and of depressive illness in close family members, particularly the mother.

Children with the acute type of depression seem to fall ill in response to some event in their lives or the lives of those close to them. Mother has had to go to the hospital, Grandpa has died, the family has moved, an especially favorite toy has disappeared—all these and many similar occurrences may precipitate an acute attack.

The distinction between acute and chronic depression flowed in large part from our observation and treatment of children ill enough to be hospitalized. In recent years our experience has increasingly widened to include outpatients, or children who do not have to go to a hospital but are treated instead in a clinic or in the doctor's offices.

In children with the type of disorder called masked depression, the sickness is very often associated with so-called acting-out behavior. This arises when a person tries to relieve or act out an emotional problem through antisocial acts that include stealing, setting fires, using drugs, running away, and beating up people, which bring on a host of related problems. Parents or others may sum up such activities by saying the child is "being bad" or has a "behavior problem."

The first two categories (chronic and acute) have remained operationally valid and been useful in our research and clinical work. However, masked depressive reaction has proved a difficult and controversial clinical entity to deal with. Almost all who have studied depressed children find severe depression very frequently associated with aggressive and somatic symptoms. If the acting-out behavior predominates and the depression seems secondary and of less magnitude in the clinical picture, the child should properly be diagnosed as having, say, a conduct disturbance, with depressive features. On the other hand, if the child fits the established criteria for a depressive disorder, that should be the primary diagnosis, with other diagnostic features stated as ancillary. In such a way the acting-out symptoms frequently will become an integral part of the depressive picture rather than a mask.

As an example of the chronic type, consider the case of seven-year-old Christine, who couldn't sleep well, ate little, and had episodes of screaming. She often threatened suicide because she thought of herself as "a bad girl" and felt that nobody loved her. The girl's mother was a helpless woman overwhelmed by family responsibilities, poor self-esteem, and a tendency toward frequent depressions. Christine had been born out of wedlock and her stepfather had spanked the girl frequently. The trouble may have started many years earlier; Christine's mother had been neglected by her own mother and brought up in an atmosphere of hostility.

One of the most important persons in Christine's life had been the paternal grandmother. Suddenly, though, when the girl was a year old, her chief care was shifted to a maternal aunt. The mother herself left Christine for several months when the girl was one and a half years old and again when she was four. Continuity of loving care makes for a stronger emotional life, and this girl had had little of it.

After Christine was discharged from our care, she again became depressed and developed abdominal cramps and diarrhea. When the mother separated from the harsh stepfather these symptoms disappeared. There is a suggestion here that the girl had been consistently afraid of him.

Six-year-old Barbara is a child who suffers the acute type of childhood depression. In her case the precipitating cause was the mugging of an older sister, 17, who had been serving as the girl's mother because the real mother worked full time outside the home. After the mugging, the sister became

withdrawn and less attentive. Within three months Barbara
was admitted to a psychiatric ward because she had gradually dropped her usual activities, slept poorly, lacked appetite, and was failing in school. Evidence that she was
markedly depressed could be found in her sad and tearful
facial expression, her monotonous voice, words indicating
hopelessness and despair, and slowness of movement.

After several days of hospital care and attention, but
with no specific treatment for depression, the girl became
outgoing and began to eat and sleep regularly. Her mood
brightened and she was sociable, active, and alert. Two
years later the mother reported that the girl was maintaining her gains.

What we once called masked depression is illustrated by
Albert, a twelve-year-old sent to us because of his disrup-
tive behavior in school. He was hyperactive and aggressive;
his grades were poor and his social adjustment marginal. A
look at the home situation suggested two probable causes: a
mother who worked away from home full time and was
unable either to provide adequate care for Albert or to find
a mother-substitute, and an alcoholic father who assumed
no responsibility for the family and who often beat Albert.
Like many others with a similar condition, the boy had
experienced both rejection and depreciation.

Throughout our interview with him, Albert was apathetic and sad. He described himself as dumb and expressed
the belief that everyone was picking on him. He saw himself as helpless. When he fantasized, he showed a strong
interest in themes of annihilation, violence, explosions, and
death—invariably with a bad outcome for the main figures.
The boys's delinquency and aggressiveness were attempts
to escape from a basic depression. Such a defense is self-
destructive, but it does help ward off the unbearable feeling
of despair—and seems to be far commoner than most of us
think.

Albert did not improve. In fact, a year and a half later, he was sent to a residential school for delinquent boys. The management of Albert's case was poor. Under the best circumstances he would have been sent to a good psychiatric facility with therapists to work with him and with his family. With excellent care, some delinquent children are able to do remarkably well. The tragedy is that depressed delinquents need much more care than the average neurotically depressed child, care not usually available. As yet, there are just not enough workers in the field who are both interested in providing such care and know how to give it. So the Alberts in this world, who need the most care, usually get the least and end up in homes for delinquents, where the outlook for the rest of their lives is bleak. They continue to live on the fringe of society and, all too often, go on to become hardened criminals.

Different Manifestations of Depression

The depressive process in children manifests itself at several different levels. The deepest level is *unconscious,* so named because the child is not consciously aware of the real meaning of what is running through his mind or motivates his behavior. He may dream, for instance, that he is being chased by a ferocious dog and cannot get away. He may wake up screaming and, when his parents ask him what is wrong, he may tell them about the dream. "It's only a dream," they may say. "Go back to sleep." But if he talks about his dream to a child psychiatrist or psychologist or someone else skilled in handling the behavioral problems of children, the counselor, by delicate questioning, may learn that in his real life the boy is scared of someone close to him—one of his parents, say, or his teacher. And his distress comes out in his dream.

There are many ways besides dreams by which an expert

can get a glimpse of what's really on a child's mind. The way a child reacts to part of a television program, or a movie, or a book, or the kind of story he tells to go along with a picture he has drawn may make clear what is bothering the child unconsciously. There are even tests specifically designed to "tap" the unconscious. One, the Thematic Apperception Test, is a series of pictures on cards. The child tells a story about what he sees in the pictures and in the telling often reveals his worries and concerns. Another test frequently used is the Rorschach, in which the child is shown a series of ink blots and asked to tell what he sees in each one. Depressive themes, as they emerge in these tests, include mistreatment, criticism, abandonment, personal injury, death, and suicide.

Another way in which the depressive process may show itself is *verbal expression*. The child may be talking or writing spontaneously or he may be responding to questions and reveal that he feels hopeless, helpless, worthless, unattractive, unloved, and guilty and that suicidal ideas keep running through his mind. When asked, the child will describe his depressed feelings just as clearly as an adult will. He will talk about feeling sad or blue or hopeless or unable to get out of bed or about not wanting to do anything.

The most obvious way the depressive process may make itself known is through *mood* and *behavior*. Here there is no need for talking; an observer can see for himself, just by watching the child, that something is wrong. Signs include sadness of facial expression and posture, crying, slowness of movement and emotional reactions, disturbances of appetite and sleep, school failure, delinquency, physical complaints for which no physical cause can be found, and, sometimes, aggressiveness.

Interestingly, when the depressive symptoms begin to fade, the signs included under mood and behavior go first.

These are the more superficial symptoms and the ones at the conscious level of the child's psychological makeup. Their disappearance is usually followed by the disappearance of depression as it is expressed verbally. Such expression is at a deeper level, the preconscious level, of the psychological makeup. The material expressed unconsciously is the last to disappear, usually only after the depressive problem has been cleared up. This material lies at the deepest level. Thus the disappearance of symptoms in depression follows a hierarchical order known since the time of Freud.

Using Defenses against Depression

Since depressive feelings are emotionally painful, children—and adults—often seek to avoid experiencing and expressing them. For example, here is young Bill, who has just lost a part-time job he had expected would keep him in pocket money until he graduated from high school two years hence. As frequently happens with Bill when experiencing a disappointment, he begins to feel depressed. But he pushes this feeling aside and goes into action. He asks his friends if they know of a job, he seeks advice from his guidance counselor, he canvasses the businesses and factories in town. Unaware that he is doing so, Bill is using the most effective type of defense: *sublimation*. Instead of moping around the house and feeling lower and lower, he is translating his concern into high-level action. Put another way, he is handling depressive feelings by diverting them into channels of which other people—and he himself—approve. Sublimation is the most beautiful and subtle of defenses. But there are many others, which Anna Freud, daughter of the founder of psychoanalysis, outlined in her book *The Ego and the Mechanisms of Defense*.

One of the most primitive and potentially dangerous defense techniques is *denial:* the depressed child simply refuses to acknowledge thoughts or feelings that are too painful. A classic example of denial is the diabetic child who will not take his insulin because he refuses to acknowledge that he has a serious physical illness. Many such children actually die because they will not use their medicine. The same is true of adults with heart disease. Denying that they have an ailment needing treatment and rest, they insist on going back to work too soon—and keel over dead.

Projection is another primitive defense. Here, something that the depressed child cannot accept in himself is projected onto—or attributed to—others. The child or adult may feel that he doesn't like somebody, but this feeling is unacceptable to him. It's easier to think that the other person doesn't like *him*. What he is actually doing is projecting his own feeling onto the other person. The most common example of projection is prejudice. In an effort not to feel inferior themselves, many people ascribe inferiority to whole groups of other people—for instance, blacks, Jews, certain nations. In other words, they project their own feelings of inferiority onto other people and act accordingly; they cannot face up to their own sense of inadequacy, so they find it elsewhere. Projection can become the basis for a paranoid view of life. People who use it a great deal go around thinking everybody's out to get them. They are less likely to be depressed than people who use other types of defenses.

In *acting out*, another type of defense, a person temporarily suppresses his depression by engaging in antisocial behavior. This may range from cheating on a test or swiping a little money from parents to setting fires or killing someone. Albert, the delinquent, could be a good example of a user of this defense.

Another commonly employed defense is *dissociation of*

affect. Here a child unconsciously represses his depressive feelings while retaining a memory of the event that evoked these feelings. Such a defense mechanism often operates after a serious loss. The child may talk matter-of-factly about an event such as death of a parent while continuing to play without any visible sign of unhappiness. Such behavior, if not understood, will appear callous to an adult and, in fact, has been used in the past as one argument against the existence of childhood depression.

At another psychological level, the technique known as *reaction formation* is often employed. Here the person talks or behaves contrary to the way he really feels. For instance, a child may dislike or even hate one of his parents. Since such feelings may be intolerable for a child with high standards, he unconsciously converts hate into love and exhibits overly friendly behavior toward the parent. Reaction formation sometimes may seem like sublimation, but unlike sublimation, it provides no pleasure and no long-term solutions.

Another common mental mechanism frequently seen in people with affective illness is *introjection.* This is the opposite of projection. The introjective type of person is the kind who feels that everything is his own fault, even when people are treating him badly. The natural dislike and hatred that he feels, he turns on himself. While the previously discussed defenses either ward off depression or mitigate its damage, introjection usually fosters depressive feelings and may often be a precipitant of the disorder itself.

All these defenses and others are used at all three levels of the depressive process described in the preceding section, that is, unconscious, verbal, and mood and behavior. At each level, the defenses have various degrees of efficiency; they do not always succeed in relieving a person of his or her depressive feelings. The extent to which the defenses work depends both on the severity of the problem the child faces and the state of his psychological or biological processes.

Maturation

In infancy the child has available only a limited number of defense mechanisms. The unconscious is primitive and does not always enable him either to contain his depressive emotions or to get rid of them. Moreover, since the infant cannot use words, he is unable to talk out depressive feelings or seek solutions to situations that induce such feelings. Unable to assess his life situation, the infant is not psychologically equipped to develop a depressive disorder as we know it in adults, which involves not only sad affect but a sense of rejection and a negative valuation of one's life situation. However, when stress (primarily loss of love objects) is overwhelming and of long duration, the infant may develop a primitive depressive state characterized by a sad face, withdrawal, failure to interact, and even refusal of food. Such primitive depressive states were described earlier in the section on pioneers in the recognition of childhood depression (see Spitz, Bowbly, and Mahler). However, even under such overwhelming circumstances, the infant's push for maturation and the ability to substitute for losses with relative ease help to counteract the depressive process. This may explain why depression in infants is often short-lived except in situations—such as the ones existing in some hospitals and other institutions—where substitutes for losses of loved persons or things cannot be found.

The toddler's growth promotes a sense of optimism, exuberance, and hope that helps ward off any sense of despair or hopelessness. Expressed another way, the push for physical growth has its counterpart in psychological mechanisms that help prevent or counteract depression.

When a loss has occurred—for instance, a neighboring family has moved, and with it a loved playmate—the toddler has a greater ability than does an adult to substitute a variety of love objects, which may be persons, places, or things, for what has been lost. This ability can lessen the impact of loss. Further, the child has a less developed ability to test reality, or to tell whether or not a given emotion or circumstance is indeed real. As a result, he or she can more readily use the defense mechanisms mentioned above and thus ward off the perception of loss. If a well-loved possession has been stolen, the child, using the defense of denial, may insist that it merely has been left somewhere. Finally, the conscience of the young child is less developed than that of older children and adults. Therefore the feelings of guilt and lowered self-esteem that may form the basis of depressive states at older age levels tend, in toddlerhood, to be less than severe. During this period, we seldom see a clearly delineated depressive syndrome but rather a variety of behavioral deviations. These deviations probably represent precursors of a variety of psychiatric disorders in childhood. We do not yet know how this matrix of behavioral deviations crystallizes into the various distinct disorders clearly diagnosable in later childhood.

In five- to six-year-old children, we begin to be able to make a diagnosis of specific depressive disorders. We attribute this to the following developmental factors. Increased intellectual development allows children to assess more properly past and future events. Attachment to a parental figure should have helped them achieve a reasonable degree of object stability. In addition, language development permits the child to clearly describe his feeling states.

In addition, a number of children from five to twelve years old, the period known to psychoanalysts as the latency stage, have to deal with an extremely harsh conscience. That's often because they have been raised by rigid or punitive or obsessional parents. A harsh conscience is the harsh parent in the child's head—or the harsh schoolteacher in his head—saying, *"Do that right or I will punish you."* Some children, including a few younger even than five, incorporate such harshness into their thinking at an early age, which makes them vulnerable to depression. As explained in the discussion of introjection, one of McKnew's young patients surprised him by saying one day, "You know, I think I have a mother in my head." It was the best explanation of introjection he had heard. This mother in the girl's head would tell her to do this and that, and when she couldn't live up to the mother's expectations she would be depressed. Not until adolescence, when they are better able to discern the real world from the unreal world, or, as psychologists put it, to test reality, do such children soften their conscience.

With the advent of adolescence, the balance of forces bearing on growth shifts to favor a breakthrough of the depressive process into words and into openly depressive mood and behavior. The growth process, which worked against depressive feelings earlier, gradually diminishes in late adolescence. Substitution for lost loved ones becomes increasingly difficult. The process of testing reality is maturing, so the tendency to use fantasy as an escape is counteracted, and the free use of more primitive defenses, like denial, is shut off.

Opposing these factors that favor the emergence of depression are more mature defenses, primarily sublimation. Other favorable factors are the ability to put one's feelings spontaneously into words, and an increased capacity to solve problems.

The APA's Classification of Depression

Adult depression has recently been reclassified by the American Psychiatric Association (APA), and the results appear in the current edition of the *Diagnostic and Statistical Manual of Mental Disorders.* This is usually referred to as the *DSM-III,* three meaning third revision.

We have made an item-for-item comparison among symptoms of childhood depression as proposed by various investigators and symptoms of adult depression as set forth in the current manual. As a result, we are convinced that the criteria generally accepted for adults can also be used, as the APA suggests, for children.

DSM-III lists three kinds of depression:

1. Major Depressive Disorder, single episode. (This is the kind we designated as acute.)

2. Major Depressive Disorder, recurrent. (This kind we called chronic.)

3. Dysthymic Disorder. This is a mild depressive disorder that was once known as a neurotic depression. (The name is derived from that of the thymus gland, which some investigators once mistakenly thought was concerned with a type of depression. The name itself does not tell anything about the kind of illness it designates.)

There is no equivalent here for what we called masked depression. As we treated more and more children and extended our research, we realized that depressive fantasy frequently occurs concomitant with many other types of mental illness and that the depressive type we called "masked" needs to be defined not so much as a distinct state but as depression per se or as a subdiagnosis in other clinical disorders. To say that a child is masking depression, we concluded, there has to be real depression, verbally expressed, under the mask of delinquency and other behavioral problems.

The *number* of children in the first two classes, which cover major depressive illness, is quite large. In the United States it probably runs into the hundreds of thousands at least. But the *proportion* of children with a major depressive illness is small. Most depressed children fall into the third APA class—dysthymic, or neurotic. It was noted in chapter 1 that the total number of American children with some type of depressive illness is at least three million and may run twice as high. In a recent epidemiological study in New Zealand, by Dr. Javad Kashani, the authors, and others, the frequency and type of depressive disorders in 650 normal 9-year-old children were as follows: prevalence at the time of the study—major depression 1.7 percent, minor depression 3.6 percent. The past (up until 9 years of age) prevalence in this group—major depression 1.0 percent, minor depression 8.5 percent.

Indications of depressive illness, as listed in *DSM-III*, include unhappiness, sadness, hopelessness, loss of appetite, disturbance of sleep, slowness of movement, loss of pleasure, low self-esteem, decreased concentration, aggressive behavior, and suicidal thoughts or actions. All of these may not be present in one person. In addition, a depressed person is likely to show disturbances in his or her school behavior. Other signs are feelings of guilt, loss of interest in life, complaints about physical illness, anxiety when separated from a loved person or thing or place, loneliness, restlessness, sulkiness, loss of energy, irritability (more likely to be found in adults than in children), and feelings of helplessness.

Wherever one looks in the history of medicine, one finds that the signs and symptoms of the illness we call depression are essentially the same. Nathan Kline says in his book

From Sad to Glad: "Depression is an ancient malady, one probably present at the dawn of history. It appears today in all societies from the most primitive to the most complex. . . . This is a natural illness, something inherent in the human condition, and not just a by-product of the anxieties created by modern times."

Symptoms alone are usually not enough to reveal the type of depression from which the child is suffering or the most promising kind of treatment. What must be known in addition to the symptoms are the history of the illness and information about school, family, and friends. The situation is a little like that with diabetes. If the patient is known to have high blood sugar, the physician can say: "This is a case of juvenile diabetes." But the physician wants to know more than that. He wants to know, for example, when the patient first becomes sick and what other symptoms he has, if these occur in connection with emotional upset, and if there is a family history of diabetes.

Rarer Kinds of Childhood Affective Disorders

The kinds of depression described so far in this chapter are those most commonly found in children. But there are some other, less frequently encountered types. One is *chronic hypomanic disorder.* The word *chronic* means long-term. *Hypomanic* refers to behavior that falls short of the intense excitement of *mania*, in which a person is overly elated, is hyperactive and agitated, and may think and talk in a grandiose way.

Tom's case is typical of hypomania. He was eight years old when he sustained a severe electrical burn. His left forearm had to be amputated, and the upper half of his body was severely scarred. He spent a year on the surgical ward of a hospital, where his mood was generally one of elation.

He was inappropriately jocular and extremely restless. He expressed grandiose ideas about his abilities, strength, and wealth but never had a complete break with reality. His hypomanic behavior increased at times of stress, such as just before an operation or when revealing his scarred body. Occasionally, there were brief periods of sadness, slowness of movement, and depression. Usually these were followed by an increase in hypomanic activity.

During the first year of Tom's life, he had been cared for largely by the maternal grandmother because his mother had to work. When he was two, his mother married and moved away from the grandmother, who had been the central figure in Tom's life. This loss was only one of many he had had to endure. A year after the accident he was admitted to the hospital's research ward for several months, where his hypomanic behavior continued. When he returned home, his feelings began to fluctuate widely. Times of family tranquillity were accompanied by a marked decrease of the hypomanic picture. However, a new stepfather, with whom he had good relations, was jailed for armed robbery, and a year later his mother was hospitalized for an acute depressive episode. Following each of these losses the boy had a long period of hypomania.

With the onset of adolescence, episodes of hypomania began to alternate with periods of chronic depressive reaction. The depressive periods were set off by realistic concerns that he was not being accepted by his peers and by worries that girls would not find him attractive. But the hypomanic picture predominated. Tom's hypomania is unusual in one respect: it was precipitated by a severe injury. More often, this rare disorder breaks out for unknown reasons during a long bout of depressive illness.

Another rare type of depression is known as *Bipolar Disorder, Mixed*. As discussed earlier in this chapter, a grownup who has episodes of severe depression may also have episodes of a condition with opposite characteristics—mania. The two illnesses are now generally believed to be different manifestations of the same underlying condition. The patient is said to be manic-depressive or to have bipolar disease.

This condition is rare but is occasionally seen in children. We treated a girl, Dora, whose development was normal until she was eleven. Then, without apparent reason, she suddenly became aggressive and overtalkative, and she boasted of sexual exploits. After several months of this behavior, which verged on mania, she became severely depressed, could not sleep, could not separate from her mother even briefly, and attempted to drown herself.

She switched into mania again, becoming endlessly talkative, engaging in dozens of activities, and in general acting as though in a state of euphoria or as if she were supremely pleased with herself and the world. Her later course and treatment are outlined in chapter 6.

Another girl, in a case described by Warren A. Weinberg and Roger A. Brunback, developed a childhood depression when she was between fifteen and twenty months old.* At the age of four she had an episode of mania. She was hyperactive and irritable, she couldn't sleep, her words tumbled out unintelligibly, and she had delusions that she was an airplane—and on two occasions "crash landed" into the wall.

The basic differences between adults and children in the manic and hypomanic states are more a matter of degree than kind. Both groups share the tendency toward grandiosity, anger, and forced joviality; however, in children these phenomena have less intensity. The children are also less

---

*Weinberg and Brunback, 1976.

likely to act out these grandiose fantasies and irrational anger. The biggest difference lies in the fact that psychotic or delusional mania is extremely rare in children, while it is relatively common in manic adults.

The Best Source of Information: The Child

In diagnosing depression in children, many authorities contend that therapists should work on the basis of information derived not only from the child but from parents, teachers, and other important figures in the child's life. Our own experience, which is not unique, indicates that there is often a disparity between the material gathered from the child and that reported by other people. This disparity seems almost unique to depressive disorders in children; it is seldom seen in other conditions. Information from sources other than the child can be important, but the child seems to us to be the most important source. We have also found that psychological testing in children—tests of their intelligence, for example, or of aptitudes or attitudes—usually does not contribute significantly toward diagnosing a depressive illness; when the diagnosis is in doubt, however, such testing may be helpful.

THREE

"I Wish I Wasn't Alive"

*A*N EIGHT-YEAR-OLD GIRL sat in her room carefully writing her last will and testament. Whatever she had, she wrote, was to go to her sister, mother, and father. She added that she loved them all. Then she picked up a rock that was almost too heavy for her to handle, carried it downstairs to where her father sat reading a book, kneeled in front of him, and said, "Daddy, would you crush my head, please?" When her father, whom she loved very much, would not indulge her in this one carefully thought-out wish, she was crestfallen. Sobbing, she ran from the house.

The father, of course, was greatly disturbed. He called to his wife, and they rushed up to the girl's room and found the note. Almost frantic, they began telephoning around and eventually reached us. We saw the family the next day and diagnosed the child as having a manic-depressive illness. This is a rare disorder among children, as noted in the previous chapter. In fourteen years of treating and studying approximately three hundred depressed children, we have encountered only four cases of it. Like this girl, three of these four children took active steps to end their lives.

Another girl, about eleven, tried to drown herself. She walked out into the ocean until she was almost up to her

neck. Then she plunged forward and let herself sink. But the waves pushed her back toward the land, and soon she was on the beach again. She tried again and again, fortunately with the same result.

A boy of about the same age tried walking in front of moving automobiles. But they all stopped in time or else managed to avoid him by swerving.

Then there was a boy, seven years old, who was depressed (unipolar). He thought he could kill himself with a pitchfork and reasoned that he could prop up the fork in a corner of the barn—prop it up very carefully so that a light disturbance, a footfall even, would send it falling. As soon as he had positioned it, he would run back a little way and then rush forward. His plan called for the fork to fall toward him, and as he rushed, its tines would pierce his stomach and he would die. But it didn't work out that way. Over and over he tried. Each time the fork fell harmlessly to the floor without touching him. Disappointed and despairing, he later related how he felt: "What a complete flop I am. I can't even kill myself!"

That's four serious suicide attempts among the depressed children we have seen, none of which succeeded. We prescribed lithium for the girl who asked her father to bash her head in. Now she's an attractive teen-ager, happy, and doing very well on that medication. The two other manic-depressive children who attempted to kill themselves—the one who wished to drown herself and the one who walked in front of moving cars—are also on lithium and doing well. As for the pitchfork fellow, he's all right too. We treated him with psychotherapy, giving him a chance to tell us everything that was bothering him and gradually getting him to see that problems *can* be overcome.

So far, we have talked only about the few cases of attempted suicide among the three hundred depressed children we have seen. But there's more to it than that. *About one hundred fifty of these children, or one out of two, had suicidal thoughts and told us about them.* These thoughts varied greatly. One child told us, "All I've ever though about is that there's no use anymore being alive." This is a mild version of the suicidal thoughts we have heard. At the more ghastly end of suicidal thoughts was the one expressed by the pitchfork boy. "If I could only stick that pitchfork through my stomach," he told us, "it would make everything better."

Suicides as Accidents

Then, too, there is reason to believe that some children killed in accidents are actually victims of suicides. There was a boy in his early teens, for instance, who had some LSD. A number of LSD users had a theory that if you swallowed some of the drug and then pulled your necktie or scarf or a rope tightly around your neck, you would get an intense sexual feeling. But this boy went into the cellar with no clothes on, stepped onto a chair, made a noose in one end of a piece of rope, tied the other end to the rafters, put the noose around his neck swallowed an LSD tablet, and then kicked the chair out from under himself. His father found him hanging there. He had been dead for some hours.

One of us saw the family. They made it very clear that the child had been distraught for a long time. They also made it clear how upset the whole family had been over various matters. They added that he was a bright youngster and had been doing well in school. There was never any question in our minds that the boy had intended to kill himself. Maybe he wanted to make it look as if he had been trying to get a sexual experience by swallowing LSD and tightening something about his neck. But he certainly had enough intelligence to know that when he kicked that chair out, there was no tomorrow. The family insisted, however, that this was an accidental death, and the coroner went along with them.

Such an event—a suicide going down in the record as an accidental death—is fairly common with adults. For example, there is reason to believe that many people killed in single-car accidents deliberately set out to take their life. Some adult patients have told us that when especially distraught they have aimed at tree trunks, hoping that after the crash they will never wake up. Or they've driven recklessly hoping for an accident that once and for all will put an end to their intense depression.

Every year an estimated forty thousand depressed people in this country kill themselves, and probably several millions of others think about it. Nathan Kline believes that the actual number of suicides each year is likely to be two and a half times as large as the estimate. That's because most suicides are not reported as such—"for religious reasons, for insurance purposes, and most often because of uncertainty, as in automobile accidents . . ." Also, Kline believes, for every suicide there may be at least ten attempts. Kline writes:

The depressive is often quite consciously guilty, and what he feels guilty about is being depressed. He has failed in his own eyes the test of will and spirit. He blames himself for his weakness, and he assumes that others blame him, too. Indeed, he often is blamed by those around him. That I believe is the overwhelming guilt that impels some depressives to commit suicide. They are driven to do something about their condition, they cannot master it, and so in one final act of resolution they end the dismal struggle.*

From Toddlers to College Students

Among college students—where the normal pressures of late adolescence are joined by such added burdens as

*Kline, 1974.

worry about taking the right course or joining the right social group, struggles to do well in academic courses or extracurricular activities, the money squeeze, the competition of fellow students—suicide ranks second only to accidents as the leading cause of death.

Very young children, too, sometimes make suicidal attempts or gestures. For example, four-year-old David wrapped himself in a blanket and set a match to it.* Just as the corner of the blanket caught fire, his foster mother discovered him. In a psychiatric interview later, the boy said he was sad because he missed his mother. He repeatedly climbed atop pieces of tall furniture and threw himself into the air, only to be caught by the therapist. Asked why he was trying to hurt himself, he replied: "Because David is a bad boy. There will be no more David." Later the therapist asked, "David, why did you try to burn yourself?" He answered, "Because I am not a good boy. David has to die." Therapist: "Why?" David: "Because my mommy wants me to."

Another boy, Jeffrey, 3, was referred to a psychiatrist because for a month he had been repeatedly throwing himself down a fifteen-step flight of stairs, sustaining many bruises. He had also been banging his head on the floor, causing bleeding. His explanation: "Jeff is bad, and bad boys have to die." During a psychiatric interview it developed that there was a new baby in the house, and "My mommy doesn't like me but likes my brother." Jeff threw a boy doll from the top of a toy truck and said, "Boy has to die."

Then there was young Benji. He had temper tantrums, destroyed furniture, and bit and pinched his foster mother. During treatment he almost stopped eating for two weeks. He bit himself till he bled, and threatened to jump in front

*Rosenthal and Rosenthal, 1982.

of cars. Then he made a boy doll fall from the dollhouse
stairs and from the top of play blocks. When the therapist
asked why the little boy was hurting himself, Benji said,
"He is a bad boy. Nobody loves him." Therapist: "Why?"
Benji: "Because Mommy and Daddy [foster parents] went
away." Therapist: "Why did they go away?" Benji: "Because
Benji was bad. Now he has to get hurt."

Benji made it clear through his play that he was afraid
of losing his foster mother, that he did not want to go to his
biological mother, and that he wanted to die.

All three of these toddlers had suffered losses—a parent
leaving or a new sibling arriving—and were craving Mother's attention. They responded with an equation often seen
in the young children we have studied: Sad=Mad=Bad.
Their self-destructive behavior served all three elements.
They attempted to relieve their loss and sadness through
attention seeking. They tried to handle their anger, rage,
and frustration through acting out. At the same time they
tried to pay for their badness, their sins, through self-harm.

Another toddler, wanting to commit suicide because he
considered himself bad, took too many aspirin. A girl of the
same age assaulted animals, other children, and her mother
and took a number of her mother's antidepressant pills.

One major study of factors in a child's life that seem
related to suicidal behavior was conducted by Cynthia R.
Pfeffer, Hope R. Conte, and fellow workers at Bronx
Municipal Hospital Center–Albert Einstein College of
Medicine.* The investigators constructed eight "Child Suicidal Potential Scales," each intended to detect and measure
a number of circumstances that might be related to such
behavior—actions that might lead to death or serious injury,
or thoughts that might do the same if acted upon.

*Pfeffer et al., 1979–80.

Fifty-eight children aged six to twelve were studied. All had undergone stress of various kinds—most commonly, worry about school failure, disturbed friendships, fears of parental punishment, or changes in the family or at school. Considerably more than half of the children—forty-two out of a total of fifty-eight—were found to have suicidal ideas, to have threatened suicide, or to have tried to commit suicide.

Certain feelings or attitudes distinguished the suicidal from the nonsuicidal children. These were: depression, hopelessness, worthlessness, and the wish to die. Also, the suicidal children were significantly more preoccupied with thoughts of death, more worried about members of their family dying, and more upset by the actual death of someone close to them. During the six months before the study began, the suicidal children were reported to have become increasingly depressed and hopeless. The mothers of the suicidal children were more frequently depressed than the mothers of nonsuicidal children. The belief that death is a pleasant state was related significantly to the degree of seriousness of the suicidal children's behavior. Also, significantly more of the suicidal children worried about doing poorly in school.

In short, this study offers strong evidence that suicidal thoughts or behavior are common symptoms among severely disturbed children from six to twelve years old. Many of the factors found to be related to suicidal thoughts or behavior in this age group are similar to those commonly recognized in adults and adolescents. The investigators maintain that a routine part of the psychiatric evaluation of children should be the assessment of the risk of such behavior.

Suicidal and Aggressive Behavior

Recently Pfeffer, now at Cornell University Medical College, has expanded the research reported above by studying the relationship between suicidal and assaultive behavior in children.* Her subjects were approximately one hundred children admitted to a hospital psychiatric ward. About one-fourth were diagnosed as depressed. The subjects were divided into four categories: nonassaultive-nonsuicidal; suicidal-only; assaultive-only; and assaultive-suicidal. Among the suicidal-only children, the most common diagnosis was depression. The greatest contrast was noted between the suicidal-only children and the assaultive-only children. The suicidal-only children were relatively well adjusted and were beset, in the main, by grief over the suicide of a loved person or by other extreme environmental pressures, such as loss of a parent or a major move. On the other hand, the assaultive-only children were marked by constitutional or temperamental difficulties such as chronic anger and assaultive tendencies, by lying, stealing, and truancy, and by bad experiences, such as those caused by parental violence.

Pfeffer speculates that suicidal behavior and assaultiveness are two independent patterns of behavior, each produced by different factors. Some other investigators, including ourselves, do not agree. Freud himself saw the aggressive component in depression as opposed to simple mourning (and pointed it out in "Mourning and Melancholia"). Such a tie between depression and aggression seems clearer in suicidal children than in most other depressed children.

*Pfeffer et al., 1982.

The infant study described in chapter 8, whose subjects are babies of manic-depressive parents, has yielded some striking findings about the relationship between depression and aggression. Many of the children show feelings toward their parents that range from indifference to love mixed with anger. These feelings are much more intense than those shown by children from homes where there is no depressive illness. The children from depressed homes also tend to control their anger poorly.

Such children can be formally diagnosed by the time they are five. As reported earlier, the children of manic-depressive parents show a rate running as high as 50 percent or 60 percent of some depressive disorders and half of these children have at least suicidal thoughts. Linda Stern, working with our research group, studied a sample of children from all social classes and diagnostic categories of depression. She found that depression appeared most often with aggression and "insecure or ambivalent attachment" to parents.

Another investigator, Dr. David Shaffer, professor of child psychiatry at Columbia University, finds that, often, suicidal behavior correlates not only with depressive symptoms, but with antisocial or aggressive symptoms. Unlike Pfeffer, he agrees with us that inwardly and outwardly directed aggression can both occur in the same individual.

Moreover, Dr. Joachim Puig-Antich of Columbia University has found that 40 percent of children with major depressive disorders also have conduct disorders. If the depressive disorder is successfully treated, the conduct disorder improves as well.

The conflicting conclusions noted above result from an honest difference of opinion. On the other hand, they could have resulted from the fact that each research team worked with a different sample of children. Our own view at present leans toward the belief that aggressive behavior and depression may occur in the same person.

Summing Up

Completed suicide is extremely rare before the age of fifteen. Even attempts are infrequent. Could gross underreporting or misclassifying be involved? David Shaffer has worked extensively to answer this question—and the answer is No.

About half of the depressed children we have seen had suicidal thoughts. But only four attempted suicide and none succeeded. We believe, however, that some children do commit suicide but that their deaths are listed as accidents—probably in large part because of family shame and because society shuns the idea that a child would take his own life.

Every year about forty thousand people in this country kill themselves. The actual number may be several times as large as the estimate, because most suicides are not reported as such.

Among college students, suicide ranks second as the leading cause of death. (Accidents are first.) But even young, bright toddlers have threatened suicide and even made attempts to carry out the threats.

Suicidal children have been found to be depressed, to have lost all hope, to feel worthless, and to have a wish to die. They thought of death more often than other children and worried more about members of their family dying. The mothers of suicidal children were more often depressed than mothers of nonsuicidal children. Often a suicidal child will also tend to be aggressive or assaultive.

How to Spot Potential Suicides

To find potentially suicidal children, two main points should be kept in mind. First, although children under fifteen almost never commit suicide, their suicidal talk and gestures should be taken very seriously. That's because these children are very disturbed and need help. In fact, their talk and gestures are usually a cry for help.

Second, children over fifteen do commit suicide, at an alarming rate, and in this age group there are really only two warning signs of suicidal behavior. One is depression, particularly accompanied by drinking or drug abuse. The other is suicidal talk. Children, like adults, almost always discuss their suicide with a friend, a family member, or a doctor within forty-eight hours of killing themselves. As of 1982, there were still no other predictors of suicide.

Incidentally, no one knows why the cutoff point comes at age fifteen—why children younger than fifteen almost never take their own lives, why children over fifteen do so rather often. It has been conjectured, however, that the younger children are more likely to receive greater protection from the family. It has also been conjectured that the younger children do not have the cognitive ability to plan their own death successfully.

FOUR

The Causes of Childhood Depression

*W*HAT SETS OFF A DEPRESSIVE ILLNESS? Presumably stress. It is known that adults who become depressed and are admitted to a psychiatric clinic have undergone a greater number of stressful events than people who have been admitted to a clinic for treatment of nonpsychiatric illness. But what are sources of stress in childhood?

Many Factors May Be at Work

Eight-year-old Dorothy was first seen by us because her mother reported that the girl had made suicidal threats. She was described as always having been sad and withdrawn, and as having much trouble separating from her mother in the normal course of becoming independent. She cried a great deal. Her father had left home when she was still a toddler but returned at infrequent intervals. Eventually the mother began living with another man. Both of these men had a good relationship with Dorothy's older brother but were very abusive of the girl. Besides abuse, anger and violence were common in the family environment. The mother, who said she herself had been unwanted as a child, has been intensely depressed most of her life.

This case history illustrates several of the factors that are found so often in the background of depressed children—rejection and depreciation, a depressed parent, and early loss of a significant person. Dorothy, when still quite young, had lost a person who was naturally of decided significance in her life—her father. Also, her father and the man who took his place rejected the girl, as shown by their abusive treatment of her. Finally, her mother had been depressed most of her own life. This circumstance suggests two possibilities. By associating with her mother, Dorothy may have picked up her mother's behavior, particularly the way she reacted to unpleasant events in her life. Or, the mother may have passed on to Dorothy biological vulnerability that made both persons succumb to depression when circumstances triggered it. Both Dorothy's environment and inherited biological makeup may have been at work here.

Sometimes only one factor appears significant. For instance, a ten-year-old girl, Betsy, was ostracized by the entire family because she was her mother's child by a previous marriage. Her inability to throw off or make light of this rejection led to a serious depression.

As these examples suggest, there are two main groups of causes of depression. In Betsy's case only one of these—environmental—seems to have been important. In Dorothy's case, a biological factor and an environmental one may have been combined.

The Family and Other Social Causes

Ten-year-old Janine lives with her mother, 31, two full siblings, and three half-siblings. The parents are divorced. We first saw Janine, an attractive but very quiet child, because she was deeply depressed and had made suicidal threats. The staff at the school where she was in third grade described her as being withdrawn, having few friends, and learning only slowly.

Her mother, a tall, slim, pretty woman, appears to be a concerned, even doting, parent. When she talks about Janine, the mother becomes depressed, and it is hard to tell when she is speaking of her daughter and when she is referring to her own lonely, depressed childhood. Her daughter's problem arose, the mother believes, mainly because the father rejected Janine and favored his other children. She speculates also that her own negative, unhappy life has somehow rubbed off on her daughter.

When Janine was ten months old she was hospitalized and then operated on for a small tumor near the surface of the brain. After three months in the hospital she came home frightened of everything. She clung to her mother and slept with her for weeks. This was the period when the mother was especially depressed and when serious conflict broke out between husband and wife. The parents separated, and the mother began going to an outside job when Janine was two. The maternal grandmother took care of the children.

Janine remained a frightened child, insisting on sleeping with the lights on, until she was six. Now she sleeps in the same room as a younger sister and is like a mother to her. She spends much of her playtime at a neighborhood recreation center but has no close friends. She often complains of headache and fatigue.

The mother says that she herself married to get away from home. She acts toward Janine and her other children much as if she were their sibling, telling them all of her problems. In front of them she tells other people that she dislikes males and hopes that her girls won't have any children so that they can escape the burdens that have been placed upon her. The mother feels hopeless about Janine's ability to lead a happy life, and she feels the same way about herself. She does maintain a neat, quiet, orderly home.

We see the mother as a depressed, dependent woman whose children are all she feels she can cling to. When she says that Janine has a problem, she's right: the child has taken into herself her mother's problem. In the words of the late Anna Freud, "They followed the mother into her depression."*

Until recent years a child like Janine almost certainly would have been misdiagnosed. Her sad mood would have been disregarded and her depression overlooked. Very often in the past such children have been felt to be exceptionally well adjusted because they were quiet and would sit peacefully, making no trouble for anyone. So the misdiagnosis was actually an appreciation of their depression and quietness—a tragic kind of mishandling. With many other depressed children, their withdrawn nature would be seen not as an indication of sadness but as a sign that they were antisocial. As a result, they would be encouraged to socialize—to mingle with other children, to participate in games and sports, to speak out in meetings. But when a therapist makes such an effort without offering help for their depression, it just makes them feel more uncomfortable than they are and worse about themselves than they already do.

The most disastrous form of misdiagnosis was to view the child as mildly retarded because his or her grades were quite poor—and the grades of depressed children often are quite poor, because a depressed youngster frequently cannot focus sufficient interest and attention on his schoolwork or on anything else worthwhile. In the past, if there were classes or schools for the retarded, the depressed child

*Freud, 1965.

who was considered mildly retarded might well be referred to one of them; consequently he might carry the label "retarded" for the rest of his life. Nowadays such a child is more likely to be placed in a special education class—where he still may acquire the "retarded" label. Hundreds of thousands of depressed children even today are regarded as normal, exceptionally well adjusted, or antisocial, or mildly retarded, and are consequently mishandled.

We often see depressed families who like Janine's ensnare their members in an abnormally tight bond that fosters unusual closeness and dependency. This has been called the "rubber fence" phenomenon. We are not talking about families commonly described as close-knit. Members of such families simply show a warm interest in one another and help one another when help is needed. They keep in touch with the other members through letters, telephone calls, birthday cards, and so on. They like to hold family reunions.

Sam's case is an example of a family with abnormally close bonds. Sam, who is ten years old, came to our attention after he had threatened to take his mother's medication when he was depressed. Sam's rather large family and various relatives all lived in the same dwelling and clung together. The boy had a fear of leaving home even to play, and other family members reinforced this fear by portraying the outside world as dangerous. His mother and an aunt were also frightened of leaving the house, so they were unable to find jobs or to make friends. Whenever Sam did go out, he would frequently telephone to see how his mother was: he was afraid she would harm herself.

In some other such families, one or more members are excluded from the family circle. Here, too, there is a rubber fence—only somebody is fenced out rather than in. In such families we often have found a striking lack of communication between the excluded members and the rest of the family. In family therapy sessions, the excluded member would sit apart from the rest of the family and be ignored not only in casual conversation but in formal therapy exchanges. When the mother of one boy who had been hospitalized for a depressive illness visited the hospital, she often sat alone in his room watching television while he played in the hallway. When he came back into his room, the mother made no effort to engage him in play or conversation. Visits were always short, and mother and son would watch the same television program without exchanging a word. This boy's mother's neglect, though she may not have seen it as such, probably contributes to his problem.

Another family pattern involves a situation in which the child is accepted provided she or he measures up to very high standards set by the family in one or more areas. Often these children are expected to excel in order to boost the family's self-esteem. Ten-year-old Frances, for example, learned to be a competent swimmer by the time she was five. The parents became increasingly involved in her aquatic activities and began to expect her to become a champion. But the girl really wasn't as talented as the family's wishes and expectations led them to believe. Each failure to win a competition was followed by the family's open expression of disappointment—and, ultimately, disapproval. The child began feeling guilty for having let the parents down and saw herself first as inadequate and then a failure. This lowering of self-esteem was followed by a prolonged period of depression.

Because family distress frequently is present in the background of depressed children, families should be evaluated. Direct and lengthy observation of the family will probably be necessary. Ideally, parents and therapists should know how to spot, before anyone becomes ill, family situations that may lead to depression. However, such expectations are unrealistic. Perhaps the school, the church, or the pediatrician could help families recognize warning signs. But, sadly, most children don't receive medical attention until they are already seriously depressed.

Separations from Loved Persons or Places

In many of our patients, frequent separations for several months or more from important people or places have taken place. These separations occurred particularly during the patients' first few years. Episodes of reattachment to the original loved person were often followed by further separations. The substitute caretakers during the time of separation were frequently indifferent to the child or provided an unstable environment. This type of loss is most commonly associated with chronic or recurrent depression.

Loss of a Strong Attachment

Often associated with chronic or recurrent depression is loss of involvement with a loved person. A central figure in the child's life suddenly withdraws his or her interest in the child while maintaining a close physical presence. The adult's loss of interest is usually related to such events as illness, personal tragedy, or new involvement with other people, as in the case of remarriage or a new baby in the home.

When there's a new baby, the older sibling often reacts in one of two ways. One that we see very often is the expression of general hostility. The older child will do everything to be bad, including messing up his or her room and thus creating trouble for Father and Mother, crying and carrying on when the parents go out, and acting like the new baby by regressing in toilet-training habits.

The second common reaction to a new baby may be called overcompensation: the older child becomes just the most loving person possible. He or she would like to kill the "little monster," but instead of showing hostility directly will coo around the baby and want to rock it and play with it. The older child will be the nicest little person possible toward the family's newest member.

Perhaps the parents will be insensitive to the older child's initial response, whether of overhostility or an unnatural degree of lovingness and goodness. In that case the child may turn his reresentment and anger inward. "If they love the new baby," he or she may think, "how can they love me? I'm worthless."

What can parents do? The best time to step in is long before the baby is born. You can talk to the other children about the new baby that's coming. You can do everything possible to try to make them part of the family process of taking in a new member. Let them listen to the baby in Mother's tummy. Take them to the hospital where the baby will arrive. Perhaps you can show them the obstetric ward and the nursery. If parents take this approach, the older children are much less likely to feel excluded. Instead they will feel more grown up and a part of what everybody is going through. Most likely they will grasp the idea that there is plenty of love to go around, that they don't have to lose anything. One of the most important features of this approach is to have older children accompany the father when he goes to fetch the baby and the mother. Then everybody comes home together. Again, the other children are made participants in the big event.

But what if this approach doesn't work? What if one or more of the children react in one of the two ways described earlier—showing anger and regression to babyhood themselves, or being so loving to the baby that everbody can see there is something phony about it?

One possible answer: don't act in a punitive way with the older child or children. It is easy to see why parents would feel like acting that way. They are tired; they are troubled. They are busy with the new baby. They've done everything they can think of to pave the way, and it doesn't seem to be working. So they get angry and say, "You can't do that!"

If parents will stop to think about it, they will realize that this is the most important time to be understanding of a little hostility, overcompensation, or regression on the part of children who preceded the new arrival. Be tolerant of the way they try to make up for lowered self-esteem and a feeling of loss. Find ways to show them special attention, such as a party of their own, an extra hug or two, permission to watch an acceptable television program a little longer. When parents act in such ways, most children can very easily weather the coming of an addition to the family.

Depreciation and Rejection

Many children with chronic or episodic depressive disorders whom we have studied have suffered depreciation or rejection by their parents or loved ones from birth onward, or at least over a period of many years. Rejection may take the form of blunt statements stressing the child's unworthiness or inadequacy, or it may be expressed more subtly through attitudes or actions that indicate a lack of respect, involvement, or caring. For instance, a parent may look at a child's report card that contains high marks in some subjects and very low marks in others. The parent makes no comment at all. He or she simply signs the card and hands it back to the child.

In some cases the parent has subjected the child to a constant barrage of criticism and humiliation. In other cases there is simply a void in the parent-child relationship: the parent's love for the child is never expressed. Since the love does exist, this is one of the most tragic situations that can occur in the relationship between parent and child.

Here we are talking about a whole range of human beings who are not very good at expressing loving feelings. They don't know how to say "I love you." They don't know how to express love around holiday times—or any other time— by sharing and giving. They don't have the ability to touch a child or an adult to show that they are caring.

Love in its essence consists not only of tenderness and caring but overt expressions of those feelings. There are many people who just can't do this. They aren't consciously doing anything bad. In their relations with other people they just have an emptiness they cannot fill. The result is particularly tragic for the children of such parents, because love to a child—or to a grownup, for that matter— is like sunshine and water to a plant. We see many children in therapy who have perfectly respectable parents. The parents really want to do the best they can. But they do not know how to express their love for the child. This is one of the hardest situations that a psychiatrist faces. Where a parent's love goes unexpressed, it may be necessary to find a relative or some other person who can supply the love the child needs. Possible candidates for such a task in addition to relatives are teachers, neighbors, scout masters, sports organizers or coaches, church leaders, and friends.

Sometimes the process of depreciation and rejection is related to an obvious characteristic of the child, such as a physical handicap. This most often occurs when the handicap is one that a parent has long been sensitive about. For example, the father may have only one testicle, and if a son is born with the same condition the father may shun him without realizing what he is doing, because he's embarrassed about his own situation and doesn't want a child who will feel as inadequate as he did. One of the fathers in the Cytryn study mentioned in chapter 1 who himself had an undescended testicle summed it up when talking about his son with the same condition, "Let's face it, he just doesn't have it."

This situation applies to many other conditions. If one parent is extremely short or extremely tall, or has long, stringy hair or is not particularly attractive, and if the unliked characteristic shows up in a child, that child may be shunned simply for having a trait the parent is embarrassed about. Sex, too, can rear its ugly head. A woman who hates being a woman will probably want only male children. If a daughter comes along, she may treat her quite badly. A child's ordinal position among his or her siblings—first, second, third, and so forth—may also influence how he or she is treated if it is the same position one of his parents occupied and if the parent was embarrassed by it. If the father was the second-born in his family and always felt overshadowed and taken advantage of by the older sibling, he may unconsciously shun his own second-born. He's identifying himself with the child who's in the same "bad" position he was in. The child reminds him of himself and makes him feel bad, so he tends to ignore him or her. This doesn't always happen, and certainly not often. But in some cases it is the underlying reason for a poor parent-child relationship that can make the child feel disheartened and eventually push him into depression.

Depreciation of the child can be shown through overprotection as well as through rejection; both attitudes convey the same basic message of the child's inadequacy and worthlessness. Telling a boy, for example, that he should not use a certain playground because "a gang of bad kids" hangs out nearby is a reflection both on his state of knowledge and on his ability to look out for himself. How much of the child's depressive outlook is caused by identifying with this negative view of himself and how much is caused by a sense of alienation from important loved ones is often hard to determine.

Depressive Disorders in Parents

The most widespread causative factor in episodic or chronic depression is depression in a parent or in someone taking the parent's place. In many of our cases at least one parent showed clinical evidence of depression, and some had been treated for depression. In others the depression was manifested as a rather subtle mood disorder that never reached a level requiring treatment.

Parental depression sometimes may be inherited by the child. Or, it may affect the child because he or she has identified with the sick parent, or because the latter's illness has lessened parental involvement with the child and this made him feel alone or rejected. Still, some of our child patients improved rapidly as soon as they were separated from their parents—a phenomenon we often observed when a child was hospitalized. Apparently this dramatic improvement occurs when the child has not taken in, or internalized, the parent's depression; in other words, he has not made the parent's depression a part of himself. In such cases the child's chronically depressed mood improved within one or two days of hospitalization and recurred only during parental visits. On the other hand, these children in whom the process of internalization seemed to be already operating remained depressed even while they were away from their parents. This was true of children as young as six years of age.

Sudden Loss

A single episode of depression is usually precipitated by the sudden and usually permanent loss of a much loved person as a result of death, divorce, or a move away from the environment the child has gotten used to. The important factors seem to be an excessive dependency on the loved person or place before the loss and the absence of an appropriate substitute afterward.

Physical Stressors

Many child patients have a physical disability themselves or have parents with such a disability. These patients include most importantly those enduring hospitalization, immobilization, pain, or disfigurement. Such children often have at least one acute depressive episode. Children with chronic disabilities—paralysis, kidney disease, severe allergies, heart disease—tend to have one or many depressive episodes or a chronic protracted depression; the frequency depends on such factors as family background, personality, psychosocial stressors, and biological makeup, which is inherited.

Children of parents with a chronic physical illness often suffer episodes of depression either because of losing the parent through hospitalization or because of identifying with the parent's reaction to the physical illness.

Social Factors in Depressed Animals

The influence of social factors in depressive illness, and particularly the presence or absence of a good parent, is clearly seen in studies of nonhuman primate mothers and their children.*

*McKinney, 1977.

In the wild, young chimpanzees who have lost their mothers commonly develop depression. First they actively protest the loss. Then they show despair, become inactive, withdraw from social life, and develop apathy. Unless older siblings adopt these chimpanzee infants, the babies usually die within a few months.* The behavior of the deprived chimp infants is strikingly like that of deprived human infants as described by John Bowlby and reported in chapter 2.

Even more revealing than such observations in the wild are the experiments with rhesus monkeys conducted by psychologist Harry F. Harlow (1905–1981) and his associates at the University of Wisconsin in the 1950s, 1960s, and 1970s. The result of one of these experiments denies, or at least throws into question, the long-held notion that babies cling to the mother and thus start a lifelong attachment to her simply because she offers them milk. Harlow separated newborn rhesus monkeys from their mothers shortly after birth and offered them substitute mothers. One of these substitutes was made of wood and covered with terry cloth. The other was made of wire and left uncovered. But this second substitute had one big advantage—a nursing bottle filled with milk from which the baby could feed.

When a baby monkey was placed in a cage with the two substitutes, he made what at first glance may seem a surprising choice. He chose comfort rather than sustenance. He spent more time clinging to the soft terry-cloth substitute than he did climbing onto the wire creation and feeding from the bottle. There is a suggestion here that, at least in monkeys, physical closeness to a mother is more important even than being fed.

---

*Because the female of the species is the primary caretaker of infants, investigators have focused their attention on the mother and child relationship. Studies of the father and child relationship in nonhuman and human species are still at the initial stage.

These monkeys raised apart from their mothers grew up to display odd sexual behavior (they felt the urge to procreate but did not know how). Moreover, the females, after they finally became pregnant, proved to be abusive and even murderous mothers. It may seem strange to anyone who has not watched a young child plead for attention, but the young monkeys that survived insisted on making contact with their abusive mothers—and on maintaining it. They did so in spite of strenuous and hurtful efforts by the mothers to keep them away. The result was sometimes surprising: eventually these mothers, worked upon by their infants' show of affection, began to be rehabilitated. They treated the babies and their later offspring much more effectively and warmly.

As noted in chapter 2, human babies separated from their mothers show signs of loss, despair, and, finally, depression. Baby monkeys do the same. One investigator, ethologist R.A. Hinde, tested infant monkeys by placing them in a strange cage with strange objects. He found that the infants who had been separated from their mother— some for six days, some for thirteen—were fearful of the objects. They were less likely to approach them than animals who had been brought up with their mothers. This effect of separation lasted as long as two years.* Other researchers separated infant monkeys from their mothers for only forty-eight hours. Even during such a short separation, all the babies showed signs of despair and protest.

Depression in children, as mentioned earlier, frequently stems from the loss of a "love object"—a person, place, or thing held very dear by the child. Something similar to this occurs in monkeys, too. A student of Harlow's, Stephen J. Soumi, raised pairs of infant monkeys together and then separated them. The result was profound melancholy,

*Hinde, 1970.

fright, and withdrawal. At ninety days, when the monkeys should have started to play, they remained sad, aloof, infantlike. As they grew older they remained fixated at the ninety-day stage of development. Earlier research had suggested that monkeys deprived of affection for as long as six months had been emotionally destroyed. But Soumi took these depressed animals and placed them in pairs with animals three months younger—at just the age when they were starting to play. In other words, he gave each depressed monkey a model of normal behavior. There were surprising results. The depressed animals gradually came out of their shells, accepted approaches, and began making approaches themselves. Before long they were engaging in uninhibited play. So far as anyone could tell, they were normal.*

Whether similar therapy would work with humans is not known. But a famous study of children who were taken from an orphanage,† where the environment was unstimulating and they received only minimal attention, and who then were placed in the care of women living in a home for the mentally retarded, is suggestive. There were thirteen such children, with an average IQ of 64. The retarded women adored them and gave them considerable attention. In two years the children's average IQ rose to normal levels, and they went on to live productive adults lives. The average IQ of twelve children who remained in the unstimulating orphanage *dropped* twenty-six points in two years and as adults they lived in the main unproductively. Children who are talked to, played with, given toys and such household objects as old pots and pans to manipulate, taken to the grocery store and on walks are much more likely than other children to grow intellectually.

Why the difference? One answer seems to be that the

*Soumi and Harlow, 1977.
†H. M. Skeels, 1966.

nature of the social environment after the separation takes place has a deep influence on the infant's reaction. For instance, where socially interested adult caretakers are present, the infant appears less likely to be upset.

Summing up, in both human and rhesus monkey babies, separation from the mother seems to induce similar results. In both cases, there is a decrease in general activity, eating, interest in surroundings, and social activities. And in both cases the final result may be death. Animal models—in particular the rhesus monkey—appear to be highly useful means for studying the depressive symptoms that often follow separation from peers or from mothers.

Telemetering Information from the Monkey

Martin Reite of the University of Colorado Medical Center points out that the higher primates, more closely than nonprimates, resemble humans in two important ways—the structure of the central nervous system and the richness and variability of behavior.* Lower animals operate on simple reflexes, or on a simple group of behaviors geared to a given situation; they do not have the wide repertoire available to humans and monkeys.

To facilitate the study of behavior and physiology in young monkeys, Reite's laboratory developed a telemetry system that can be implanted in the monkey's body and that sends back information on body temperature, heart rate, eye movement, and muscle activity, and three measurements of the brain waves. Because of this development, information about the monkey's physiology can be obtained while the animal is engaged in normal activities unrestrained. In addition, the animal's behavior is videotaped.

*Reite, 1977.

In preliminary work, the Denver research team has studied some twenty infant monkeys, about half separated from their mothers for four days and the other half for ten days. Telemetry units had been implanted in them when they were five or six months old, and the units were turned on after they had recovered from surgery. The investigators recorded baseline observations for several days; then they separated the mother and the young offspring. Immediately after separation, the baby monkeys began behaving in an agitated manner and their heart rates shot up. These heart rates remained above normal through most of the first day of separation and then began dropping. As the separation continued, there was a tendency for the heart rate to return toward normal.

Sleep habits changed markedly the first night of separation. The animals spent more time awake, awoke more often, and spent considerably less time in so-called REM (for rapid eye movement) sleep. In REM sleep the eyeballs move constantly though the eyes are closed. In humans it is known that during such periods the sleeper is dreaming. As separation continued, most of the monkeys returned to their normal patterns, but REM periods remained abnormal till the mother was returned.

Like heart rate, body temperature rose during the period of agitated behavior, which lasted much of the first night. This behavior was followed by evidence of depression, which continued throughout the separation. Usually beginning during the first night and continuing to the end of separation there were significant drops in body temperature, both night and day. The levels returned to normal following reunion with the mother. There were also changes during the separation period in the brain waves as recorded on the EEG (electroencephalogram).

The mechanisms underlying these various changes have

not yet been determined, and comparable measurements of depressed humans are being studied. The hope is that researchers will be able to isolate specific biological state markers whose presence accompanies a depressive episode and whose absence accompanies improved mental health.

Biological Factors in Depression

Clearly, many instances of depressive episodes and even of chronic depression can be traced to some psychological or social stress. But is this stress sufficient in itself to set off a depressive attack? Or must there be a biological weakness—a predisposition to depression—waiting to be set off? May this biological vulnerability, presumably inherited, be sufficient in itself to cause depressive illness in at least some persons? Or does it always have to be triggered? What is the nature of this weakness? Questions like these have been asked increasingly in recent years, and much research has been done—mostly with adult patients—in an effort to find answers.

Nature of the Biological Abnormality

If a predisposition or a tendency to develop a major depressive illness is inherited, as it seems to be in a great many cases, the question of *what* is inherited becomes important. Something could have gone awry in some of the billions of neurons that constitute the brain's gray matter, or in the functioning of some other part of the body, or in the way certain parts of the brain or the rest of the body interact.

So far the chief clues point to brain chemicals called transmitting agents or neurotransmitters. These agents help carry messages from neuron to neuron. Within each neuron, or nerve cell, the message is transmitted electrically. But between one neuron and the neurons next to it are tiny gaps called synaptic clefts. A message coursing through a neuron bridges the gaps with the help of the chemical transmitting agents. There are many such agents, of which the best known so far are norepinephrine, dopamine, and serotonin. These are closely related compounds, the first two belonging to the chemical family known as the catecholamines and serotonin to the family of indolamines (figure 4.1).

According to the *catecholamine hypothesis** of the biology of depression, something goes wrong with the amount of the transmitting agent available at the synapses. (Several things *could* go wrong. For instance, the neuron making the agent may not supply enough of the neurotransmitters to carry the message to the next neuron. Chemicals [enzymes] that break down a transmitting agent after it has served its purpose may go to work too fast, so not enough of the agent is left in the gap. Or the neuron may produce too much of the agent. These are three of the many possible mechanisms.) When there is not enough of the agent in the synaptic cleft, according to this hypothesis depression results. When there is too much, the outcome is mania. Scientists have investigated the catecholamine hypothesis for about twenty years without being able to confirm it. But they have made some intriguing findings. For example, chemicals that are effective against depression or mania alter the amount of brain catecholamines.

A competing explanation is known as the *serotonin hypothesis.†* The theory is that a deficit in the amount available leads to depression, and an excess to mania. One major piece of evidence is the presence of low levels of serotonin's

---

*Schildkraut, 1965.
†Coppen et al., 1965.

4 • 1 THE CATECHOLAMINE HYPOTHESIS

The brain is made up of billions of nerve cells, or neurons, that "talk" to each other by means of chemical compounds called neurotransmitters. Produced by the neuron, they act as the brain's messengers, carrying a message from one neuron to another. They are highly implicated in changing an individual's moods and behavior.

In this schematic, we see one neuron (a) releasing transmitters into the synaptic cleft for absorption by another neuron (b). Precise regulation of the body requires a rapid "turn off" by the receiving neuron (b) so as not to absorb too much of the transmitter substance. This is achieved by a process known as reuptake. That is, some of the transmitter is sent back to the neuron (a) that originally released it whereupon it is broken down chemically by an enzyme. The catecholamine hypothesis suggests that when these processes are malfunctioning—for example, when too little of the neurotransmitter norepinephrine becomes available—the individual becomes depressed. (See pp. 122–40 and figure 6.1 for the effects of antidepressant drugs on these processes).

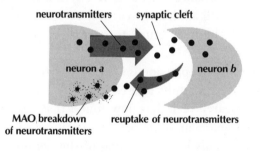

neurotransmitters   synaptic cleft

neuron *a*   neuron *b*

MAO breakdown   reuptake of neurotransmitters
of neurotransmitters

---

major breakdown product in the spinal fluid of depressed people and also in the brain tissue of depressed adults who committed suicide.

In contrast to the large amount of biological research on adult depressive illness, such research with children has only recently begun. The few studies that have been done provide some evidence of a common biological link between adult and childhood depressive illness. For example, some depressed children respond much the same way as adults to antidepressant medicines. This may be an indication that the underlying trouble in both depressed adults and children is the same.

Some Other Biological Effects

Cortisol is a hormone secreted by the adrenal glands and associated with stress reactions. In the evening and early morning, its secretion stops in normal adults but continues in depressed patients. These patients excrete more cortisol every twenty-four hours than normal persons. Just why this happens or what effect it has on patients is not yet known. One investigation has now demonstrated that some preadolescent children with major depressive illness have a similar disturbance of the daily rhythm of cortisol secretion.[*] As with adults, the cortisol excretion patterns of the depressed children return to normal upon recovery from depression.

Then, too, depression is associated with a variety of sleep disturbances in adults and children. A University of Minnesota research team has now found that one sleep disturbance common in adult patients occurs also in depressed children.[†] This is a shortening of the period between the time a person goes to sleep and the time he begins dreaming, or the onset of REM sleep. If a normal sleeper is awakened during a REM period, he or she if asked will start telling about the dream that has just stopped. There are five or six such periods during the night, and they account for at least one-fifth of a person's sleeping time. While the shortening of the time before dreams begin, called a decreased REM latency, is the only sleep oddity noticed so

*Puig-Antich et al., 1979.
†Kupfer et al., 1970.

far in depressed children, adult patients have been found to experience additional disturbances of sleep. Depressed adults sleep less than normal persons, and they awake earlier. Also, the amounts of time they spend in each of the various stages of sleep differ from that of normal persons. So far the report of a sleep disturbance that is common to both children and adults who are depressed is based on only a few studies. But that finding and the one about cortisol secretion strengthen the theory that in depressed children as in depressed adults, biological changes occur.

The Genetic Risk

Unless you are a close relative—meaning a parent, a brother or sister, or a son or daughter—of a person with the most serious kind of depression, you have less than one chance in one hundred of developing the disease yourself. We are talking here about the major forms of affective illness, namely bipolar and unipolar. If you are a close relative of such a patient, you have about a 20 percent to 25 percent chance of developing the condition yourself sometime in your life.

Studies of twins have proved highly useful in uncovering the genetic role of many illnesses. This is particularly true of studies of pairs of identical twins, each of whom has the same inheritance because both twins developed from the same fertilized egg. In the case of major affective illness, such studies have found that if one identical twin is affected the other is also affected, or becomes affected, in from 50 percent to 100 percent of the cases. The findings are quite different in studies of fraternal or nonidentical twins—who do not have the same inheritance, because they have developed from *two* fertilized eggs. Here the chance of both twins developing an affective illness ranges from no chance in some studies to as high as 40 percent in others.

David Rosenthal* studied several hundred young men and women in an effort to learn whether heredity or environment was more important as a cause of major illness. Some of these were children of a parent with a manic-depressive or schizophrenic illness who had been given up for adoption at an early age. Others were adopted people whose biological parents were free of major psychiatric illness. A third group was comprised of children whose own parents were mentally healthy but who had been adopted and raised by couples, one of whom was either manic-depressive or schizophrenic.

Rosenthal and his fellow workers were able to make a number of interesting comparisons. The gist of their findings was that in the transmission of manic-depressive disorder and schizophrenia, heredity counts for far more than parent-child relationships or, by implication, environment in general. The sick young people with a biological parent who was psychotic had the most severe disorder. This was true whether they had been raised by the families into which they were born or by foster parents who were free of major mental illness. However, when a young person had become ill in spite of the fact that his parents were not psychotic, there was a distinct and much stronger relationship between the severity of the illness and the quality of the adoptive parent-child relations. The poorer the relationship, the more severe the disorder.

Such findings are evidence of a strong genetic factor in adult affective illness. But they do not rule out the possibility that in some cases the disease is caused at least in part by the conditions under which a person is raised or by some other factor in his life. For instance, one manic-depressive

* Rosenthal, 1970.

adult became sick only after he had almost completely and without warning lost his hearing. Possibly he had inherited a predisposition to bipolar affective disorder; if so, the loss of hearing served to trigger the illness.

In sum, childhood depression may be the result of social or biological factors or both. Social factors include either loss of or rejection by a loved one. Rejection doesn't necessarily mean that the child is actually ignored or pushed out of the loved one's life. It can also mean that someone simply fails to give him the warm attention and love that he needs for his best development. Social factors also include the family. A family whose members are abnormally close to one another and fearful of the world outside can foster depression in a youngster. So can families who set goals too high for their child. Depression may be associated, too, with a physiological disability suffered either by a child or a parent. Underlying all of these causes of childhood depression may be a disorder in the child's biological makeup—something that may be inherited and thus make the child predisposed to depression. In adults with major affective illness, heredity has been implicated in a large proportion of cases—as high as 100 percent in some research—but an inheritable biological abnormality has not yet been specifically identified.

FIVE

Who Is at Risk?

NOBODY IS CHEERFUL all of the time. Everybody goes through low periods, when he or she takes a gloomy view of what's going on, wonders whether the sun will ever shine again, questions that there are any really good things in life—and if there are, that he or she can ever attain them.

In that sense, everybody is at risk to depressive moods. But such moods are ubiquitous. Unless caused by the loss of a loved one, or a move from loved surroundings, they rarely last more than a week, if that. And even when they have been occasioned by a deeply felt loss, they rarely linger more than a few months to a year.

What we are talking about here and in most places throughout this book is the depression that persists or is recurrent—the kind that constantly interferes with a child's usual life, with eating and sleeping, play, school activities, and/or conduct; neither a "stage" through which the child is passing nor a passing change of mood. It is more serious and pervasive—something that the child does not seem to be able to shake without assistance.

What *"At Risk"* Means

If your parents or brothers and sisters have heart disease, you are considered at risk to the same ailment. If they have diabetes, you are at risk to diabetes. Both of those conditions, as well as many others, have a strong hereditary element.

You can also be at risk for environmental reasons. If you work with certain chemicals, you are more likely than most other people to get cancer. If you work in a mine, or if you smoke cigarettes, you are more likely, on the average, to get lung disease.

Being at risk means that you have a higher probability of coming down with something than somebody else. You are in a situation where the probability of being afflicted by a given condition is greater than it is in the general population.

People who are at risk to mental illness are in this position for basically one of three reasons. One reason is that the condition runs in their families, so they may have inherited a predisposition to it. Another reason is that they were raised in a very disturbed family. In this case no genes may be involved, just a disturbed environment. The third reason is more general. A person can escape genetic problems and a disturbed childhood but be at risk because of other circumstances in his life. If a person marries someone who becomes emotionally disturbed, he is at risk to a diastrous marriage, to a lowered standard of living because of medical bills and time lost from work, and even to becoming disturbed himself. If a person gets along very well with the boss and then the boss dies and is succeeded by someone who is difficult to get along with, he is at risk both to unemployment and to emotional disturbance, including depression.

Children with a Depressed Parent

The children most at risk for the more serious type of depressive illness are those whose parent has a major affective illness. This does not necessarily mean that the child inherits the illness or a predisposition to it. The child may simply adopt or copy the depressed thinking and activity of the parent as he copies many other parental behavior patterns. By doing so the child may become depressed himself; in short, he learns to be depressed.

But in many cases the parent's depression is actually inherited by the child in the usual sense of the word. Geneticist Elliot Gershon and his associates at the National Institute of Mental Health (NIMH) examined 524 first-degree relatives (direct blood relatives) of people in Israel having psychotic depression.* Of these relatives, 49 had some form of major depressive illness, as compared with only 4 relatives of 619 normal controls. In other words, there was about ten times as much serious depressive illness within families containing some depressed people as within families without such depressed members. Moreover, depressed patients had about eight times as many relatives with moderate depression or with so-called cyclothymic personality, in which periods of moderate depression and moderate elation occur regardless of what's going on outside the affected person.

Some years ago we studied thirty children, aged five to fifteen, of fifteen patients who had been hospitalized either for unipolar or bipolar illness.† We saw the children twice, four months apart. Of fourteen boys, five were diagnosed as depressed both times we saw them, and three were diagnosed only once as depressed. Of the sixteen girls, four were

*Gershon et al., 1976.
†McKnew et al., "Offspring," 1979.

diagnosed both times as depressed, eleven only one time. (Here the Weinberg criteria were used; see chapter 2.) To put it simply, roughly one-third of the children who had a parent hospitalized for affective illness were themselves rated depressed.

A further study using the same methods brought similar results.* But this time the conclusions could be firmer because the study included not only children of affectively ill parents but controls, or children whose parents were emotionally well. Of the thirteen families in which at least one parent had a major affective illness, eleven had one or more children who on at least one interview were depressed. In contrast, of the thirteen control families only three had children who at any time were depressed. When the same children were evaluated using the more stringent *DSM-III* (see chapter 2) rather than the Weinberg criteria, the results were very similar.

It seems fair to conclude, then, that children who have at least one parent with a major affective illness are at greater risk for a depressive disorder than children whose parents are emotionally well. The increased risk may be caused by inheritance or by living with a mentally ill parent. It should be mentioned that most of the depressed children in our second study had a minor form of the illness (dysthymic disorder), none were psychotic, and none had symptoms of mania or even hypomania, a condition in which a person is often excited, elated, or angry, but never to the point of mania. This was so even though thirteen of the fifteen parents were bipolar. The widely held notion that manic symptoms in childhood are rare was thus supported by our studies.

Following the study, we wondered whether the depres-

*Cytryn et al., "Offspring," 1982.

sive states we had found might be only a transient or passing phase. They could simply represent a reaction to having
a depressed parent, particularly one who was hospitalized.
But this conclusion does not rule out a genetic predisposition in some children, even those we did not judge to be
depressed. For example, one of the children was depressed
only one time when we saw him at the age of thirteen, yet
he developed a psychotic mania at fifteen and responded
well to lithium.

Recently we studied eighteen of the children seen in our
first study.* At the time of the original study, the mean age
of the children was ten years. At the time of the follow-up
study, their mean age was fourteen years. To interview them
we chose investigators who did not know how either the
children or the parents had been previously diagnosed. As
in the previous studies, each child was interviewed twice,
four months apart. The interviewer determined for each
child whether or not he or she met the Weinberg criteria
for depression. In addition, the interviewer diagnosed each
child according to the *DSM-III* criteria.

Originally, twelve of the eighteen youngsters had been
diagnosed as depressed according to the Weinberg criteria
on either one or both of the two interviews. This time seven
of those were depressed on one or both of the interviews
according to Weinberg or *DSM-III* criteria. Of the remain-
ing five, three had some type of psychiatric disorder. Among
the conditions were Overanxious Disorder, Conduct Disorder, and Obsessive-compulsive Disorder. Only two of the
children rated depressed at the time of the first study were
considered free of any psychiatric disorder at follow-up. Of
the six youngsters not originally diagnosed as depressed, five
were considered free of psychopathology at follow-up and
only one had a major depression.

* Apter et al., 1982.

In conclusion, our study indicates that children who are significantly depressed, if untreated have an unfavorable prognosis, at least in adolescence. Almost half of the children we studied were depressed on follow-up, and most of the remainder went on to develop a variety of other nondepressive emotional disorders as evaluated by *DSM-III*. The hopeful note is that the children who were free of depression in childhood continue to enjoy relatively good mental health during adolescence. Because of the consistency over time of the psychopathology or its absence, it seems of paramount importance that childhood depression be taken with utmost seriousness and be vigorously treated.

In a similar study,* Elva Poznanski and her colleagues followed ten children aged twelve to twenty-three who six and a half years earlier had been diagnosed as depressed. They found that 50 percent of these children were clinically depressed at follow-up and that none of the remainder were free of psychopathology.

Because children of parents with affective illness represent a group so clearly at risk, any psychiatrist or other therapist evaluating or treating such *adults* should inquire about the emotional status of the patients' children. We have often found a family interview, including all family members, to be revealing. Moreover, all child psychiatrists and other practitioners, when seeing depressed *children*, should inquire about the possible existence of a similar disorder in the siblings or parents.

We should like to emphasize that by no means do all children of depressed parents themselves become depressed. Though they are said to be at risk to depression, many live completely normal lives. It is tempting to describe at least some of these as invulnerable: they apparently have not inherited anything that predisposes them to the illness, and

---

*Poznanski et al., 1976.

they have managed to steer clear of or to fend off the potentially detrimental influence that a depressed parent can have.

Invulnerable Children

This concept of invulnerability has received considerable attention among investigators of schizophrenia. For example, psychiatrist E. James Anthony of Washington University in St. Louis has pointed out that when an invulnerable child turns up in a family with a schizophrenic parent, he or she is likely to have had little contact with the ill parent for whatever reason.* Such a situation allows the child to avoid overidentification with the sick parent.

The child who is likely to come down with a schizophrenic illness, according to Anthony and his followers, is the child who is close to the sick parent. This child often acts as a caretaker of the parent and, by doing so, seems to hasten the process of identifying with her or him. Anthony tells of a family whose schizophrenic mother would never eat at home because she feared someone was poisoning the food. The father and son would not accompany her to restaurants because they did not share her belief. Though the daughter may have been skeptical, she humored her mother and ate wherever she ate. The son stayed well. The daughter, after entering college, began showing signs of schizophrenia, the result perhaps of genetic influences as well as those factors described above.

The same process seems to be at work with affective disorders. We first noticed this when we were seeing the families of the depressed children under our care. If one of the parents was depressed, the child we were treating often was close to that parent. In a family interview, the child would sit next to that parent, often clinging to him or her,

---

*Anthony, 1972.

in many cases looking quite as depressed as the depressed adult, whom the child was very dependent on but at the same time made special efforts to protect.

We realize that the above issues may cause considerable concern among readers who have an affective illness and worry about their offspring. It is important to keep in mind that most affective disorders are episodic in nature, and people with even major disorders can expect lengthy periods of good emotional health. During such healthy periods most affectively disturbed people function well and often are unusually warm and empathic. This latter circumstance can go a long way toward compensating for difficulties encountered during the periods of illness. In addition, spouses, siblings, and other relatives may serve as important buffers and sources of emotional support during periods of parental illness.

Hyperactive Children May Also Be Depressed

Hyperactivity, or, as it is often called, Attention Deficit Disorder, seems to increase the likelihood that a child will develop, or already has developed, a depressive illness. Typically, hyperactive children cannot remain quiet. They are marked by restless and aggressive behavior, difficulty in concentrating, and problems in doing schoolwork. Often they have learning disabilities and are clumsy. Most have signs of minor neurological impairment that would account for many of their behavioral difficulties. The typical hyperactive child is into everything. Some few hyperactives are involved in antisocial activity, such as stealing, truancy, or generally acting out. Usually, hyperactive children cause distress at home and in school by their continual restlessness and their inability to concentrate.

At least some hyperactive children are now believed to be depressed. This is because when hyperactives have been seen in psychiatric clinics they have often been found to rank low in self-esteem, have feelings of being worthless and helpless, feel unable to control their lives, and feel isolated from their peers. These symptoms are generally shared by depressed children. Of twenty-seven hyperactive boys aged seven to twelve who were seen at the University of Missouri by Walid Shekim,* eight, or 30 percent, were diagnosed as depressed, according to strict criteria. These hyperactive children with depressive symptomatology excreted relatively low levels of a urinary metabolite of catecholamines (see chapter 4) known as 3-methoxy-4-hydroxy-phenylethene glycol (MHPG), a finding noted in other groups of depressed children.

The relationship of hyperactivity to depression in children is not yet fully clarified. Among the two most likely possibilities are: 1) that hyperactive children develop a secondary reactive depression in response to the many hardships incurred by their illness, that is, school failure, lack of friends, family conflicts, disappointments; and 2) that hyperactivity and depression may have a parallel etiology and coexist in the same child as autonomous entities.

Delinquency and Depression

Javad Kashani of the University of Missouri, in collaboration with the authors, studied 100 boys and girls aged eleven to seventeen who had been incarcerated by the court in a juvenile justice center in central Missouri.† Of these, almost one-third had a depressive disorder, the most common symptoms being a feeling of sadness or unhappiness, sleep disorders, and changes in appetite. The first two symptoms were exhibited by every one of the depressed

*Shekim, 1980.
† Kashani et al., 1980.

adolescents. The girls exhibited a much higher incidence of depression than the boys. When examined prior to being committed to the institution, however, the youngsters had a rate of depression seen in normal populations. There are two theories to explain the sudden and drastic change. The more obvious one is that life in a juvenile justice center is not exactly a happy experience. The other possible explanation is that the delinquents' capacity to act out their impulses had been taken away by the structure of the institutional environment. Many youngsters can't stand losing this capacity and defend against this loss of freedom by becoming depressed.

The Sex Factor in Depression

There is a common belief that women are more likely than men to become depressed. If one is talking about all kinds of depression, that seems to be true. Among people with neurotic depressive illness, or, as it is now called, dysthymic reaction or minor depression—a reaction to some traumatic event in a person's life, such as the loss of a job, or a forced move—women outnumber men by a ratio of four or five to one. The reason is not clear, unless it is assumed that men are emotionally tougher or less sensitive than women and are less affected by environmental events. The other explanation may be that women are given tacit permission by our society to express their feelings freely, while men are expected to be stoic and unemotional. Another factor may be the female sex hormones, which are clearly related to mood disorders, as exemplified by premenstrual depression and postpartum depression. With the more serious types of affective disorders—unipolar and bipolar disorders—the story is different. They affect males and females in equal numbers.

Social Class

Much more mental illness occurs among poor people than among those who make up the middle and upper classes. There are more schizophrenics among poor people, more depressed people, and more manic-depressives; in fact, almost all diseases (physical and mental) show up with greater frequency among poor people than among the wealthy. The reasons are most likely environmental. Poor people have to contend not only with poorer housing, clothing, and food but also with poorer medical care. They have access to fewer services for their babies, both before and after childbirth. The person born into a poverty-stricken environment has less opportunity to rise and in many respects must struggle harder than his opposite number in the better-off classes simply to live. Moreover, as Nathan Kline points out, well-educated persons from good backgrounds are more likely than the poor to admit emotional trouble and get psychiatric and/or medical help in time for it to do the most good.

Other Groups at Risk for Depression

In chapter 1 we indicated that the impetus for one author's study of childhood depression was the frequent finding of depressive symptoms in chronically ill and handicapped children. Such findings have since been confirmed by many psychiatric and pediatric investigators. In addition to the conditions previously named as existing concomitant with depression, others have been added, such as epilepsy, burns, asthma, diabetes, colitis, and leukemia and other forms of cancer. It stands to reason that the depressive states and other forms of psychopathology seen in these groups (anxiety, acting-out behavior) are a reaction to one's difficult or hopeless life situation.

Another group neglected in terms of their feelings are the mentally retarded. It is true that the severely retarded are very difficult to assess psychologically; however, among the majority, who are only mildly retarded, there are many, especially during adolescence, who develop depressive symtoms and even a depressive disorder, which may seriously compound their already marginal functioning.

Childhood depression is far from being completely understood, but we do know several factors that seem to be instrumental in its development. The most important is the presence of a parent who is afflicted with a major affective illness. A predisposition to this illness can be genetically passed on to the child. Exactly what biological process is responsible for the predisposition is not yet known, but it may lie dormant in the child unless spurred to life by some source of stress in the child's environment—grief over the loss of a loved person or thing, or a number of other factors, discussed in chapter 2. However, even without environmental stress the gene can become expressive at a certain age.

Parental depression can affect a child even if a predisposition is not transmitted genetically. This is because most children try to identify with their parents and tend to copy and be influenced by parental behavior. If the parent is depressed and the child copies his or her behavior, the child may become depressed as well.

Most children with depressed parents do not themselves become depressed. Though some may have inherited a predisposition to the illness, their family and other people who influence their lives are in general so understanding and loving that nothing happens to light the fuse that sets off the disease. Also, most children learn that the behavior of a depressed parent is sick or at least unhealthy, so they refrain from copying it.

The most hopeful note on the influence of parental depression on children is that drugs have been developed to check depression and allow the parents to live normally, particularly if the medicine is accompanied by psychotherapy.

Our work suggests that a sizable proportion, perhaps half, of depressed children remain depressed through adolescence at least. Most of the others develop some signs of less serious mental problems, if not depression.

Hyperactive children, as well as delinquent children and those with chronic illness, handicaps, and mild mental retardation are more likely than normal children to be depressed.

We have been talking throughout this chapter of children who are at risk for depressive illness. But being at risk does not mean that a child who happens to be in a certain category of children is bound to develop depression. It only means that his chances of doing so are greater than average. Still, we believe that there is no reason for alarm, because childhood depression for the most part, as discussed in the next chapter, can be treated simply and effectively.

SIX

What to Do about It: Treatment

*I*F YOU SUSPECT that your child or someone under your care is significantly depressed for a period of at least several weeks, what can or should you do?

The first thing is to confirm your suspicion by consulting the child's pediatrician, your family physician, or the school nurse or counselor. These sources may either alleviate your worries by diagnosing the child's condition as a harmless, passing phase, or they may refer you to a child psychiatrist, psychologist, child guidance clinic, or community mental health center for further study. The better that one of these sources knows the child and the family, the more effectively and quickly administered treatment will be.

If professional help is recommended two kinds of treatment can be sought. One is psychological treatment, or psychotherapy, and the other is pharmacological (drug) treatment. The two are often used in combination.

Goals and Types of Therapy

The all-encompassing goal of therapy is to help the patient reach the highest level of functioning he is capable of, while alleviating mental pain or anguish. This goal may be reached through *insight*, *behavior modification*, or *counseling*. These general types, along with specific examples of their application, are described below.

Probably the most commonly used form of psychological therapy is analytically oriented psychotherapy. This therapy is based on the premise that people's emotional difficulties arise from largely unconscious conflicts that lead to distorted views of oneself and others accompanied by painful feelings. This form of therapy, whether used with an individual, a family, or a group, has a common base of operation: to evoke insight into personal difficulties, provided the patient is intellectually and emotionally ready for it. Perhaps more importantly, it makes use of what has been called the *holding situation* by British child analyst David Winnicott, which refers to stability and consistency in the therapist-patient environment. Therapists who employ this type of treatment use what psychiatrist Edward Strachey, in the 1930s, called the *mutative interpretation*, which encourages the patient to express all the bad things he feels about himself. Then, he projects these feelings by attributing his bad characteristics to the therapist; or if he's receiving therapy in a group, he may also project them on some group members. The therapist and/or members of the group interpret to him his largely unconscious maneuver and by doing so give him back a corrected, realistic version of his often distorted ideas and feelings. If this process is sufficiently repeated, he can gradually begin to change and acquire a new idea or picture of himself and of the people in the world around him.

Another general method of psychological treatment is behavior modification. It is based on various learning and behavior theories that hold that human behavior is not governed by unconscious forces but, rather, shaped by specific environmental factors. Behaviorists stress environmental factors that influence behavior and pay little attention to insight or other intrapsychic factors discussed previously. The emphasis is on manipulating environmental conditions in order to alter certain behaviors. Behavior alteration is often achieved by reward and punishment systems. So-called positive reinforcement involves a system of rewards that may be tangible, such as food, money, or candy, or intangible, such as privileges or praise. Negative reinforcement seeks the extinction of undesirable behavior. The most common techniques used toward this goal include purposefully ignoring a specific behavior or administering some form of punishment.

A variant of behavioral therapy is the so-called cognitive therapy, as developed by Aaron T. Beck and modified for use in children by Maria Kovacs at the University of Pennsylvania. The basic assumption is that emotional disturbances, including depression, are caused by distortion in thinking on a conscious level. The disturbed thinking of a depressed person, according to this theory, includes three major elements: 1) negative self-esteem; 2) negative view of the past and present; and 3) hopeless outlook for the future. Cognitive therapy attempts to correct this disturbed thinking by direct logical examination of the patient's views, thus helping him to gradually adopt a realistic view of himself, his environment, and his destiny.

The ultimate goal of any therapeutic intervention will vary from case to case, according to many factors. Some therapists and patients seek to relieve the present symptoms without attempting to alter the patient's basic personality characteristics. Others may be more ambitious and strive toward the realization of the patient's full potential. Such strivings may be limited by the severity of the patient's past and present life circumstances and by the extent of the patient's motivation and determination to seek change. Sometimes even the most motivated patients and their families are frustrated by mundane circumstances, such as the availability of treatment, and monetary and time considerations.

The child psychiatrist or other child therapist can choose from a number of types of treatment that usually are most useful in the earlier stages of the disorder. The most important of these is some kind of family intervention. This can include intensive family psychotherapy, in which all family members are encouraged to discuss what they know about the problem and the circumstances that precipitate it and are guided to see how changes in their own behavior may alleviate it. It can also include periodic counseling of the parents, with or without direct contact with the child.

Working with Families

All work with families calls for certain amounts of insight therapy and certain amounts of guidance, and children and parents may benefit from both. We've seen some patients for years and never given them a piece of advice. With other patients, almost the entire time of every therapy session is taken up with advice giving.

The choice of method will depend on the severity and length of the illness, the age of the child, and the intelligence, motivation, and insightfulness of the parents. The younger the child, the more responsive she or he will be to environmental changes alone. For example, a change in the amount of time that the mother or father is available to the child can be extremely helpful.

Parent Counseling

Mental health professionals sometimes see families who are not aware of the potential harm to the child of some of their child-rearing methods. Recently one of us has been dealing with a family that farmed out a child all week to a grandmother and brought him home for the weekend. The mother, coming herself from an emotionally deprived background, had a lot of difficulty understanding the traumatic effect of this arrangement. In such cases it is often not feasible to help the parents by interpreting the child's feelings of rejection; rather, the therapist has to be directive and point out to the parents the relationship between the child's life situation and his depression.

Other advice to the parent about the child may include, for example, taking him during the weekends on outings, fishing, or picnics. During the week, taking the child on shopping trips, to the library, or helping him with his homework may be suggested. All activities will bring the parents closer to, or more in touch with, the child. The therapist may also suggest to the parents that they help the child cope more effectively with specific depressive issues that have arisen in the child's life. If there has been a recent death, the family will be advised to talk about it with the child openly and to answer frankly any questions he may have. Grief may be lightened by being brought out in the open. If the child is depressed about not having friends, the parents may be advised how to go about teaching and helping the child make more friends—through such strategies as joining in a game at the playground, inviting children to a party or a cookout at home, or asking someone the child likes particularly to go to a movie as a guest.

Where the child is older, in grade school, or when depression is of long duration or great intensity, work with families should include the affected child and, often, other family members as well. In such cases, family therapy often has to be supplemented by individual work with the depressed child and with the parents—particularly if, as so often happens, one or both parents are depressed. Whenever it can be used, a form of therapy that interprets what is going on but does not direct the family in so many words what to do is most efficacious, in our experience, in producing long-term benefits. That's because it leads to insights about things going on within the family and how one can make one's life better fit the family's needs.

When the therapist tells the family to spend more time with the child or to stop sending him away during the week, he is using direct guidance. But when the therapist tries to get the family to understand the process of scapegoating, in an effort to decrease depreciation and rejection of the child, he is using insight therapy. In scapegoating, the child is blamed for virtually every untoward event that occurs. Naturally the child's self-esteem is negatively affected and low self-esteem is a cardinal mark of depression. With some families, the therapist can help undo this process. He can get them to see that scapegoating makes a child feel worthless, inhibits his natural desire to accomplish things, and makes him wonder if life is worth living. When the child's family members come to realize this through insight, they are more likely to abandon the scapegoating pattern than if they are simply given direct advice such as: "Quit complaining about this child," or "Knock off blaming the child for things he didn't do." A person who reaches conclusions on his own is more likely to act firmly than a person who has been told what to do by someone else.

The same process of insight therapy can work where the child is depressed because of a major loss. The therapist can help the family understand that such an occurrence may affect a child more deeply than an adolescent or an adult because the latter two have more interests and usually more understanding friends to offer emotional support. The therapist may also explain that because of inexperience a child may feel that the loss of a favorite friend or relative means the loss of all hope. Given these insights into the situation, many families can come to their own conclusions about what to do to correct it.

Parent Therapy

If a parent has a depressive illness, it is very important to provide appropriate treatment, in order to improve the parent's functioning and thus to furnish a nondepressed model for the child to follow and identify with.

Individual Therapy with the Child

In some cases of childhood depression, family and parental treatment may not suffice and individual psychotherapy for the child may be indicated. The specific goals in such a circumstance differ only somewhat from those set up for adult patients. The crucial one is the development of a close, empathic, and trusting relationship with the therapist. In addition to good professional qualifications, the therapist has to be an intuitive person sensitive to the child's needs. Many distinguished therapists, such as Dr. David Levy and Dr. Frederick Allen, have even gone so far as to say that such a relationship accounts for most successes achieved in psychotherapy with children. All would agree that it is the cornerstone of such therapeutic work.

Second in importance is what Dr. Franz Alexander calls a corrective emotional experience: the child experiencing a different and more healthy response from his therapist than he had experienced earlier in his life. The therapist accepts the child in his totality without criticism or judgment. Where appropriate, he expresses approval of the child, which is often in contrast to the previously experienced constant disapproval. Since low self-esteem and hopelessness are the hallmarks of childhood depression, the therapist has to make special efforts to convey to the child that he values him as a person regardless of shortcomings and has firm hopes about the child's ability to overcome his difficulty in becoming a well-functioning, self-respecting person.

A third important element is encouraging the child to ventilate all his negative feelings and thoughts—fears, worries, sadness, hopelessness, conflicts with important people, anger, and distortions of himself and others. Although Anna Freud stressed that such ventilation is not sufficient,* it is important that the child feel free to get things off his or her chest with appropriate affect in a nonthreatening and supportive situation.

As with adults and families, advice and counseling play important roles. Such devices may include encouraging the child to attempt new relationships or repair old ones that went awry because of misconceptions grown out of depressed feelings. Therapists and parents as well can encourage children to get into things they are known to be good at. If they have been good at sports, they can be encouraged to become involved in athletic activities. If they have been good at or shown interest in musical activities, school dramatics, photography, dancing, the school newspaper, or any other activity, they can be encouraged to take it up. Participation in such work and play is a marvelous way of increasing the self-esteem and psychological strength

*Freud, 1929.

of a depressed child. The therapist may also talk over with the child a particular troubling situation and try to get the child to see what he or she can do to overcome it. For example, if lack of help with difficult homework is a cause of depressed feelings, the therapist can suggest how the child can go about asking a parent, brother, sister, or schoolmate for help with a particularly troublesome assignment. Or, if the child is concerned about lack of playmates at home, the therapist may suggest asking the parent's permission to have friends over in exchange for doing chores around the house.

The final goal is helping the child to understand the basis of his or her feelings and conflicts. With the help of the therapist, the child has to learn to understand his or her unrealistic perception of himself or herself and others, his or her neurotic conflicts, and the alternative ways available to him or her to cope with his or her life circumstances in a more effective and adaptive manner.

Sometimes all the above techniques fail because of the truly hopeless nature of the child's situation. In such cases it is crucial that the therapist acknowledge such a reality and help the child to cope with it. The therapist may say: "It's clear that you can't do anything with your mother (father, sister, and so forth) that would help her to be more caring about you or like you more." Such statements indicate that a caring mutuality exists in the interpersonal relationship between the therapist and the child, which may be the main hope for improvement in such a situation.

Although the goals of therapy are basically the same for all children, regardless of age, the technique employed obviously has to be tailored to the child's chronological age and the degree of his or her cognitive or emotional readiness. In our experience, children as young as five or six can talk about and discuss their difficulties in a reasonable manner and require a minimum of nonverbal activities such as play or games to clarify their problems. But younger children require play therapy, which employs dolls and other play materials and games. Through play the child can express in his or her own way all the problems older children verbalize more directly. The level of interpretation also has to be adjusted to the age of the child.

In conclusion, we emphasize that in our experience most depressed children respond favorably to psychotherapy. One of our major allies responsible for this success is the maturational push children experience, which makes it easier for a child than an adult to change and mature (see chapter 2).

Community Collaboration

There are many cases, of course, where family conditions make traditional psychiatric intervention infeasible. In such cases, the therapist may have to work with community resources such as schools, juvenile courts, halfway houses, foster homes, and the police, on behalf of his depressed patients. In the course of treatment of depressed children, we have often gone to schools for meetings with the teachers, arranged for care in halfway houses or foster homes, talked to the police, and testified in court.

Hospitalization: A Way to Intervene in a Crisis Situation

For the vast majority of depressed children, hospitalization is *not* needed. The children who need hospitalization all have a major depressive disorder, are acutely ill, and are unable to function in their usual surroundings at home or school. In such cases, although hospitalization may at first seem frightening, it is really beneficial to the child. In an appropriate hospital situation—we are thinking of a large, modern hospital with a department or ward appropriate for seriously depressed youngsters—the children soon adjust to their new surroundings.

One of the most fascinating findings of our research to date has been the relatively prompt and sustained improvement of even chronically depressed children whom we admitted to hospital research wards.* This was entirely unexpected, since we anticipated a temporary worsening of the depression as a result of separation from home and family. Improvement took place despite the absence of any formal in-hospital treatment program. It was almost universal in children with acute depressive reactions and was frequently seen in those with chronic depressive reactions but almost never in children suspected of having masked depressive reactions. We believe that this phenomenon is due to the removal of the child from an often noxious environmental situation, coupled with the rallying of the family around the child who is labeled ill because of the hospitalization. In a five-year follow-up we found that many depressed children sustained the improvement initiated in the hospital, despite the fact that some patients did not subsequently avail themselves of therapy. Progress was most dramatically evident in several cases of chronic depressive reaction.† Our experience should encourage people to consider the possibility of brief hospitalization of depressed children as an effective form of crisis intervention.

Some investigators report cases of hospitalized children who do not recover as rapidly and spontaneously as the children we have just described. For these children a more prolonged hospital stay and the use of medication may be necessary. However, it should be stressed that such cases are very rare.

*Cytryn and McKnew, 1982 (*Medicine et Hygiene*).
†Cytryn and McKnew, 1982 (*Medicine et Hygiene*).

Drug or Pharmacological Therapy

In recent years, there has been a greatly increased use of drugs in the treatment of depression in adults. Very recently, drugs have also been used against depression in children, and although only tentative answers are in as to their usefulness it looks as though they are going to be as helpful with children as they are with adults.

However, we strongly feel that if drugs seem necessary for a depressed child they should never be used as the only method of treatment but, rather, in conjunction with psychotherapy. Our stand is based on an observation made by a number of therapists: that in many adult depressed patients drugs alone may not be sufficient to bring about adequate improvement. Almost all adult patients respond to a combined use of drugs and psychotherapy, and there is increasing reason to believe that the same is true of children. If a child is sufficiently disturbed to require drugs, he needs psychotherapy, too, to help him understand and work through the disturbing and sometimes even terrifying experiences he has been through while ill.

Use of Drugs in Adults

Three basic groups of antidepressant drugs are now in use for adults: tricyclic drugs, the monoamine oxidase (MAO; an enzyme) inhibitors, and lithium. In general, the first two groups are used to treat unipolar illness, in which the patient may be severely depressed but does not become manic. Lithium is used principally against bipolar illness, in which the patient alternates between periods of depression and mania, and which is believed to be rooted in a biological vulnerability. Many patients with unipolar illness also respond to lithium. In such persons the unipolar illness is believed to be virtually the same as the bipolar disorder—and to have similar biological roots—but to manifest itself differently. We have mentioned the minor depressions (see chapter 2), where the disorder may have no biological foundation but, rather, represent a reaction to a stressful life situation.

Commonly the three groups of drugs are used in the following ways:

Against unipolar illness • Most clinicians treat this condition with either tricyclic drugs or MAO inhibitors. However, if a unipolar patient has a family history of bipolar illness, he or she would be treated with lithium. The latter will also be used if a unipolar patient fails to respond to the other antidepressants. Sometimes, the optimal treatment is to combine lithium with a tricyclic drug or MAO inhibitor. As we have mentioned (see chapter 5), recent research findings lead us to believe that unipolar and bipolar disorders are different manifestations of the same genetic disorders. Based on these findings, some clinicians now advocate the use of lithium as the initial drug in both unipolar and bipolar illness.

Against bipolar illness • Most patients with this disorder are in a manic or hypomanic state by the time they reach a physician. If the patient is extremely agitated, the first medicine prescribed is usually a tranquilizer, most often Haldol, a member of the phenothiazine family of drugs, which is then followed after a few days by lithium. When patients are in a less disturbed condition, they are given lithium, to which most respond very well.

Against neurotic depression or minor depression • The biological and genetic factors in minor depression are not yet clearly understood. Most people believe that this form of depression represents a reaction to something stressful in the environment, such as death, loss of a job, or marital problems. The drugs used here are the tricyclics and MAO inhibitors—*not* lithium. The tricyclics are the medicines of choice. The MAO inhibitors have also proved excellent for people who have what psychiatrists call depressive personality, meaning that they have been depressed to some extent for many years and the depression rarely lifts, even for short periods.

As described in chapter 4, the neurotransmitters, norepinephrine and serotonin, facilitate the transmission of messages in the nervous system. To the best of our knowledge, tricyclics and MAO inhibitors are effective because of their interaction with the neurotransmitters. The tricyclics are believed to block the reuptake of norepinephrine or serotonin into the nerve cells that released it, where it would be deactivated or destroyed. The MAO inhibitors work by blocking the action of the enzyme, whose job is to break down the neurotransmitters (figure 6.1). Thus, both groups of drugs work in different ways to keep more of the neurotransmitters active in the synapses, or spaces between cells.

The exact action lithium takes in affective disorders is unknown. However, two theories have been proposed. One stresses the action of lithium on the movements of two electrolytes, sodium and potassium, in and out of the nerve cell. The second theory suggests that lithium deactivates or destroys norepinephrine and thus makes it less available at the synapse, eliminating the surplus of neurotransmitters believed to underlie manic disorders. This latter theory does not facilitate our understanding of lithium's effectiveness in treatment of some unipolar depressions.

Electroshock treatment is often used with affectively disordered adults who are acutely ill but do not respond quickly enough to drugs. It is usually successful, though no one knows exactly the mechanism involved. There is some

6•1 EFFECTS OF ANTIDEPRESSANT DRUGS

Two types of drugs, MAO inhibitors and tricyclics, are used to treat affective illness. They appear to work by increasing the amount of neurotransmitter in the synaptic cleft.

Under normal conditions the neurotransmitter substance crosses the synaptic cleft, where some is absorbed by the neighboring neuron (b), while the remainder returns to neuron (a) (reuptake), where it is chemically broken down. This allows for proper mental and physical functioning (see pp. 91–95 and figure 4.1). Sometimes, not enough of the neurotransmitter substance reaches the receiving neuron (b). The catecholamine hypothesis suggests that this decrease in absorbed neurotransmitter substance brings about depression.

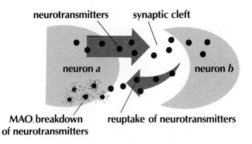

MAO inhibitors aid by inhibiting the breakdown process, thereby making available more transmitter substance to return to the receiving neuron (b). The tricyclics, another group of drugs, inhibit the reuptake process. This action also keeps more neurotransmitter substance available. In both cases, the underlying idea is to regulate the amount of transmitter substance in order to reach a proper balance.

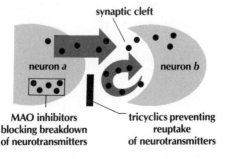

evidence that it affects the action of neurotransmitters. Since drugs and psychotherapy work well with children, there has been no need as yet to use electroshock.

Imipramine

One of the most widely used drugs for depressive illness in adults—and coming into use in childhood depression—is a tricyclic, imipramine. A Swiss doctor, Roland Kuhn, accidentally discovered its value against depression in 1956 while looking for a drug that would be more effective against schizophrenia than one of the major tranquilizers, chlorpromazine. The compound he was testing turned out to be ineffective against schizophrenia but an excellent antidepressant. It was imipramine, marketed as Tofranil. Several related (so-called tricyclic) drugs have also proved efficacious in treating depression.

MAO Inhibitors

The same year Kuhn was discovering the value of imipramine, Nathan Kline was working with iproniazid, an MAO inhibitor, which had been developed to treat tuberculosis. This drug made people with tuberculosis feel elated—sometimes *too* elated, in fact—and made them mentally more alert. When Kline gave iproniazid to depressed patients, he got similar results.

Within a year, hundreds of thousands of patients were treated with the new medicine for depression (marketed as Marsilid), usually with good results. However some patients developed jaundice, a few developed high blood pressure, and others developed severe reactions to certain foods while on the medicine. So iproniazid was withdrawn. But it led to the development of other drugs having similar beneficial effects and less serious side effects. Parnate is the trade name of the one most commonly used.

Lithium

Lithium is most useful in treatment of bipolar illness, though it is often used also in cases of major depression. This dual role for lithium exists based on the fact that, as we have mentioned, the two types of mood disorders have similar biological mechanisms and share a common hereditary basis, though their manifestations are different.

In its pure form, lithium is a very soft whitish-gray metal. One of the basic elements, it was discovered early in the last century. Combined with carbonates, citrates, chlorides, and other such substances, it is known as a salt. In 1949, in fact, it was offered as a substitute for table salt (sodium chloride) in salt-restricted diets. The results were bad. Several patients afflicted with heart trouble died, and many with heart or kidney disease were poisoned. So the use of lithium virtually stopped.

Oddly, it was in that same year, 1949, that an obscure Australian physician, John Cade, published a paper reporting a great discovery he had made about lithium—to which scarcely anyone paid any attention. Working in a crude laboratory in a small hospital, Cade was trying to test his idea that psychosis was caused by some toxic substance in the body. He injected urine from four groups of people—persons afflicted with mania, depression, or schizophrenia, and normal persons—into guinea pigs and noted the results. Some of the animals were not affected; the rest developed convulsions and died, whether the urine had come from sick or well people. The urine from some of the manic-depressives was especially powerful. Injected in quantities only one-third or one-fourth as large as samples from other persons, it paralyzed and killed the guinea pigs.

Now, what was the toxic agent? Cade eventually suspected uric acid and decided to administer it in pure form—combining it, however, with a solution of lithium salts. By doing so, he could more readily control its potency. He reran the experiment, this time supplementing the injections of urine with one of the uric acid and lithium combinations. Surprisingly, all the injections proved to be far less toxic than the first time. Next, following an obvious trail, he injected lithium alone. It had a strong tranquilizing effect. The guinea pigs, when placed on their backs, instead of squealing and kicking as usual just lay calmly. They were lethargic.

A simple association of ideas led Cade to try lithium on manic-depressive human beings. It was the urine from such patients that had proved the most powerful in paralyzing and killing guinea pigs, and it was lithium that had calmed these restless animals. He used a group of subjects that included schizophrenics, depressives, and persons in the manic stage of manic-depression. He got the expected results: lithium had little or no effect on the people with schizophrenia or depression, but it produced tremendous improvement in those with mania. Cade wrote about one typical manic:

> This was a little wizened man of 51 who had been in a state of chronic manic excitement for five years. He was amiably restless, dirty, destructive, mischievous and interfering. He had enjoyed a preeminent nuisance value in a back ward for all these years and bid fair to remain there for the rest of his life.
>
> The patient commenced treatment on March 29, 1948. On the fourth day the optimistic therapist thought he saw some change for the better but acknowledged that it could have been his expectant imagination; the nursing staff were noncommittal but loyal. However, by the fifth day it was clear that he was in fact more settled, tidier, less disinhibited and less distractable. From

then on there was steady improvement so that in three weeks he was enjoying the unaccustomed and quite unexpected amenities of a convalescent ward.*

After two months he was discharged and resumed a normal life at home. He took a small maintenance dose of lithium carbonate. Six months later, though, he was back in the hospital, as manic as ever. It turned out that he had felt so well that he had stopped taking his medicine. He went back on it and got well again.

Cade's report was virtually ignored for some years, particularly in the United States, where lithium was a bad word because, as recounted earlier, it had once been used as a salt substitute and had killed several people who had heart disease. In the mid-1950s in Europe, however, a spirited campaign in favor of lithium's use was begun by a noted professor of biological psychiatry at Aarhus University, Denmark—Mogens Schou. He had discovered Cade's reports, tried lithium himself in manic-depressives, found that it was indeed efficacious, and begun enthusiastically to spread the good news. His reports were picked up in New York City by Drs. Ronald R. Fieve and Ralph Wharton, who, with their associates at the New York State Psychiatric Institute, tried lithium on manic-depressive patients. Through the 1960s, however, it was restricted in the United States to experimental use, though it had been adopted in many other countries—40 or more—in Europe, Asia, and Africa. In 1970 the Food and Drug Administration, acting on the recommendation of a lithium task force of the American Psychiatric Association, approved the use of the drug in this country to treat and prevent mania and manic-depression.

Lithium is particularly a godsend because it seems to get

---

*Kline, 1974.

at the heart of the trouble endured by many of the world's most creative people in a wide variety of fields, people who suffer from bipolar illness or manic depression. During the highs they work brilliantly and almost tirelessly. But, after a time—days, weeks, months—they almost invariably become psychotic or fall into the trough of depression. For varying periods, then, they require hospitalization or another form of seclusion. Given prophylactically, lithium often prevents the recurrence of extreme highs and lows.

Mania and Creativity

One of the most interesting stories we know about manic-depressed persons and lithium is told by Dr. Ralph Wharton, who was among the first physicians to use lithium in this country. It's about a patient of his who was a highly creative artist. His trouble was that he could only create while in a manic state, which he did not know until after lithium had smoothed out his highs and lows. He came to Dr. Wharton one day and said something to the effect of: "I can't create anymore. I have to get into one of my highs."

He and the physician worked out an extraordinary arrangement. Late in the spring Dr. Wharton would take him off lithium, and the artist would go to some far place with a close friend and proceed to have what was essentially a controlled breakdown. Watched over by his companion, he would go into a manic state, his creative powers restored. When he had finished the work to his satisfaction, he and his friend would return and see Dr. Wharton. Very carefully, then, the physician would put him back on lithium, and the man would become stablized, happy, and content—fit once again to mingle with other people. He was no longer as creative but he was in good shape to go around selling his creation. And next spring he could repeat the process.

The story of another highly creative person, one who associated himself publicly with lithium at an American Medical Association symposium, is quite different. He is Joshua Logan, American playwright, theatrical director, and producer, who told the following story.*

"My first impression was that something had sneaked up on me. I had no idea I was depressed, that is mentally. I knew I felt bad, I knew I felt low. I knew I had no faith in the work I was doing or the people I was working with, but I didn't imagine I was sick. It was a great burden to get up in the morning and I couldn't wait to go to bed at night, even though I started not sleeping well. But I had no idea I had a treatable depression. I had no idea it was anything like a medical illness. I thought I was well but feeling low because of a hidden personal discouragement of some sort— something I couldn't quite put my finger on. If anyone had told me that I could walk into a hospital and be treated by doctors and nurses and various drugs and be cured I would have walked in gladly and said, 'Take me,' but I didn't know such cures existed. I just forced myself to live through a dreary, hopeless existence that lasted for months on end before it switched out of dark-blue mood and into a brighter color. But even then I didn't know I had been ill.

"My depressions actually began around the age of thirty-two. I remember I was working on a play, and I was forcing myself to work. I couldn't work well. I directed a very elaborate musical comedy on Broadway, and on a pre-Broadway tour during the time I was in this depression. I can

*From pp. 42–47 in *Moodswing: The Third Revolution in Psychiatry*, by Ronald R. Fieve, M.D. Copyright ©1975 by Ronald R. Fieve. By permission of William Morrow & Company.

remember that I sat in some sort of aggravated agony as it was read aloud for the first time by the cast. It sounded so awful that I didn't want to direct it. I didn't even want to see it. I remember feeling so depressed that I wished that I were dead without having to go through the shame and defeat of suicide. I couldn't sleep well at all, and sleep meant, for me, oblivion, and that's what I longed for and couldn't get. I didn't know what to do and I felt very, very lost. I remember I asked a friend of mine who was with the company manager to walk around the block with me during lunch because I didn't want to have to converse with the cast lest they sense my feelings. I told my friend that the play was awful. He said, 'No, no. It's not so bad. I don't know what's the matter with you, you're looking at things wrong. Come on now, just buck up.'

"It seemed to me that all friends of the average human being in depression only knew one cure-all, and that was a slap on the back and 'Buck up.' It's just about the most futile thing that could happen to you when you're depressed. My friends never even hinted to me that I was really ill. They simply thought that I was low and was being particularly stubborn and difficult about things. If anyone had taken charge and had insisted that I go to a mental hospital, I probably would have gone straight off. Instead, they simply said, 'Please don't act that way. Please don't look at your life so pessimistically; it's not so bad as you think. You'll always get back to it. Just buck up.'

"Finally, as time passed, the depression gradually wore off and turned into something else, which I didn't understand either. But it was a much pleasanter thing to go through, at least at first. Instead of hating everything, I started liking things—liking them too much perhaps. I swung into a different mood altogether, which I didn't understand; nor did anyone else. At first people thought I was drinking, even though I was seldom around any bar, and I wasn't seen to take a drink of alcohol in front of anyone, so they couldn't quite explain it that way. And yet I was fairly flamboyant in my thoughts, imagination, and speech without really being dangerous. I was certainly very active mentally and physically. I lost weight, dropped down almost overnight to my best weight, like a fighter in good trim. I put out a thousand ideas a minute: things to do, plays to write, plots to write stories about.

"I decided to get married on the spur of the moment. I pursued a girl, talked to her a lot, and talked persuasively to her parents. I swamped them with favors. She was so beautiful and lovely that I practically forced her to say yes. Suddenly we had a loveless marriage and that had to be broken up overnight.

"By this time even my mother, sister, and family doctor were quite certain there was something wrong. One day two psychiatrists from a nearby hospital in Westchester [New York State] were sitting in my apartment when I came home. One of them said to me, 'You're in the midst of a very serious nervous breakdown.' This was my first major state of manic elation, that at first had seemed so pleasant and productive. At that point I wasn't sleeping at all. Whether I needed it or not, I didn't want to be curtailed or put into a hospital. I can only remember that I worked constantly, day and night, never even seeming to need more than a few hours of sleep. I always had a new idea or another conference. I directed another play which should have taken at least a month or five weeks. I directed it in two weeks, including two previews. It was a revival of the famous old farce *Charley's Aunt*, which is a pretty manic play to begin with. And it introduced to the world Jose Ferrer, who has a high-flying quality about him, always. It also introduced me to my present wife, who was to play the real aunt. It was an exhilarating time for me. I was extremely productive, perhaps overly so, but it was the best thing I think I've ever done in my life. I doubt if I've ever had the freedom of thought and unfettered ideas which really connect with an audience that I had during that time.

"When the notices came out, I was considered 'discovered'. They had never talked about direction in any of my plays until then. Suddenly I was a famous man, and I was shot into an even higher mood state. It finally went too far. In the end I went over the bounds of reality, or law and order, so to say. I don't mean that I committed any crimes, but I could easily have done so if anyone had crossed me. I flew into rages if contradicted. I began to be irritable with everyone. Should a man, friend or foe, object to anything I did or said, it was quite possible that I could poke him in the jaw. I was eventually persuaded by the doctors that I was desperately ill and should go into the hospital. But it was not, even then, convincing to me that I was ill.

"There I was, on the sixth floor of a New York building that had iron bars around it and an iron gate that had slid into place and locked me away from the rest of the world. I had made a deal with the doctor who had finally got me into the hospital. He had had to promise that I would not be put into any special ward or be locked up in any way. I looked about and saw that there was an open window. I leaped up on the sill and climbed out of the window on the ledge on the sixth floor and said, 'Unless you open the door, I'm going to climb down the outside of this building.' At that time, I remember feeling so powerful that I might actually be able to scale the building. I was in a psychotic high. They immediately opened the steel door, and I climbed back in. That's where manic elation can take you.

"Over the succeeding years, including four in the army, I had mild mood swings, but no major disruptions. During this part of my life and later, I had a course of psychotherapeutic and psychoanalytic treatment with Dr. Lawrence Kubie. He turned out to be a great friend and helped me with many of my own personal problems that had grown out of my hospitalization and my extraordinary success. Without his help, and the help of several other psychiatrists, my freedom to express myself may well have been curtailed. But a few years later, without apparent warning, I again found I was getting ill. This time I was doing a play with an important cast. All through this period I had been doing plays—in fact, my most successful ones. *Mister Roberts* and *South Pacific* were written during a happy period, but I felt nowhere near as high as I had been when I was really in a manic state. I was happy with my work, but never manic until many years later—thirteen years after my first hospitalization—when I was directing this new play. Suddenly, I had so many things crowding in on me, including a new movie career that was starting, and I found that again I was ill. This time there was a crisis in my work. I left the play and went to a hospital in New Orleans where I was given electroshock treatments—six of them—and came out in a very short time, better than when I had gone in. After that I went through years of work in pictures and plays when sometimes I was slightly high and productive, and sometimes I was slightly low. But by this time they had begun to learn about various drugs.

"I visited psychiatrists three and four times a week, and at various times I took antidepressants to elevate my mood and tranquilizing drugs to reduce it. But it was only toward the end of this last career of mine, which was mostly in motion pictures, that I began reading about lithium, which might actually stabilize the highs and lows that I had suffered from for years. I have now been taking lithium carbonate for four and a half or five years, and I've not been

conscious of the slightest highs or lows out of what would
be considered a normal proportion. And yet, I seem to be
as productive as I've ever been. I've collaborated this past
year on two different musical comedies, and I'm writing
my own autobiography. It's been a rewarding and enjoy-
able experience."

Treating Children with Drugs

While Europeans such as Eva Frommer began using
drugs with depressed children many years ago, they
employed few if any control groups, and their diagnostic
criteria were unclear, making their results difficult to interpret. Recently Joachim Puig-Antich and his colleagues
started administering imipramine to children with a major
depressive disorder, with good results.* The doses ranged
from 1.5 milligrams per kilogram of weight to 4.5 milligrams per kilogram of weight. The improvement was grad-
ual, becoming significant after three or four weeks on the
maximum dose.

True, there were some side effects. These included dry
mouth; nausea; constipation; sleepiness; tachycardia, or
irregular heart beat; and anorexia, or loss of appetite. That's
why this drug—and all other antidepressants, for that matter—has to be given under the direction of a physician and
the physician has to keep close watch on the patient.

Many doctors feel that the tricyclic drugs, when given
in high doses, as they often have to be in children, may
adversely affect the child's heart function. Safer drugs, we
believe, will be coming along. However, the tricyclics do
work and are probably safe, with careful monitoring, especially of heart function.

---

*Puig-Antich et al., "Plasma levels of imipramine," 1979.

We are not aware of any attempts to date to administer MAO inhibitors to children. However, with their increasing use among adults, one may expect them to be tried with children as well, particularly in those who are unresponsive to tricyclic drugs.

As with other forms of drug therapy, lithium has been used only recently in the treatment of children, mainly because manic or hypomanic states in children are very rare and often go unrecognized. Children reportedly responsive to lithium include those who are hyperactive, undergo cyclical mood changes, exhibit aggressive behavior, and have explosive outbursts. It may be found eventually that all of these conditions are early manifestations of bipolar disorders, or manic depression, in which lithium, as we noted above, proves particularly effective. Our own ongoing study indicates that children with bipolar disorders respond well to lithium. We'd like to tell about two of our cases.

Marilyn was eight when she was brought to us on an emergency basis by her mother, a professor at a nearby university. She had always been moody, her mother said, had had a number of serious depressive episodes, and had gone through several high periods, when she didn't sleep well at night and was overbusy and overexuberant. Because the mother had a bipolar illness herself and had done well on lithium, she suspected that her daughter might be developing a manic-depressive disorder. The situation became critical when Marilyn made a suicide attempt (see chapter 3).

When her mother brought Marilyn to us, the girl was markedly depressed. We weren't worried too much about her suicide potential because it has been our experience that eight-year-olds may talk about suicide, but as a rule do not carry through. So we did not hospitalize her, especially since both parents were most responsible and cooperative.

Instead, we involved her in a research program we had started in order to learn what types of children responded to lithium. We were giving children lithium for four weeks, followed by placebo for four weeks, and then taking them off and, finally, giving them lithium again. We would repeat this procedure several times in order to make sure that the children who responded were indeed responding to lithium and not just the fact that they were in the program or were hearing things from us that may have been unintentionally therapeutic.

Every time Marilyn got lithium she responded to it; she became noticeably and definitely less depressed. And every time the placebo was substituted for lithium she became very depressed again. After the research program was completed, we put her on lithium on a regular basis. That was about six years ago. Ever since, except for two episodes when she stopped the lithium on her own—as most patients do because they think they don't need it any more—Marilyn has remained on lithium. The times she stopped taking it, she became quite depressed and had to come see us again and get started on her medication. She has done marvelously well and is now a most personable and well-adjusted teen-ager. If ever there's a walking proof that some children do develop a full-blown bipolar disorder at a very young age, she is it. She's also a walking advertisement that lithium works with at least some children just as well as it does with adults.

The other patient we'd like to mention is a girl named Dora, who was eleven years old when brought to our attention. She had been having mood swings—more pronounced than Marilyn's—for about a year. During a manic period she would stay up most of the night, writing letters to her friends and reading books; during the day she would participate in every school activity for which she could possibly find time. She was a cheerleader, tried out for one athletic team after another, worked on the school newspaper—was in fact so overactive that the school staff became distressed. She was the closest to a true manic state that we have seen in a child. Alternating with these highs, she had serious lows, during which she would be very depressed. There were no episodes so dramatic as Marilyn's taking a rock to her father and requesting him to use it on her, but Dora had attempted to harm herself (see chapter 2).

Dora, like Marilyn, was put into our lithium research program and responded well. She has been maintained on lithium for some years and is now a successful adolescent who is functioning at a very high level and is grateful for having been treated. Like Marilyn, she stopped her medicine several times because she felt she no longer needed it. Each time, she became depressed, returned to see us, was put back on lithium, and soon was doing well again.

Most children who respond to lithium get clearly better in from four to seven days. However, the work that has been done so far in using lithium with children can be described only as most tentative. In contrast to experience with adults, our studies confirm earlier reports that side effects in children are relatively rare. However, neither the ultimate safety of lithium in children nor the size of the maintenance dose (the dose necessary to prevent relapses) has been definitely determined. It would seem prudent to avoid using lithium where the patient has kidney, cardiovascular, or thyroid disease; to periodically screen the thyroid and kidney function; and to use caution in determining how long to use the medicine.

Lithium has proved itself in adults. Unquestionably, it does prevent suicide and enhance the quality of life for many people. All except about 15 percent of patients taking lithium as a prophylactic or preventive drug no longer have major attacks of depression or mania. There is, certainly, a great deal of controversy about it, but the controversy centers on such questions as whom exactly to use it with, under what circumstances, and for how long. A study of biological rhythms now going on at the National Institute of Mental Health and elsewhere may eventually enable us to predict when a person is likely to have a major attack of depression or of mania and thus permit us to reduce the dosage of lithium or prescribe it for the times when it will do the most good. Side effects, such as the tremor and nausea that adults have noticed, might then be eliminated. As for children, we are just beginning to learn its possibilities.

Drugs or Psychotherapy?

Against major affective disorders, the best treatment currently being offered combines psychotherapy and psychopharmacology. Psychotherapy alone in these conditions has not been found to be particularly helpful in many cases. However, combining drugs and psychotherapy, especially in the most serious depressions, is more efficacious than using either method alone. We are talking here about adult patients. However, in the same disorders the same thinking would apply to children. With Marilyn and Dora, who had bipolar disorders, we used psychotherapy as well as lithium. Dr. Puig-Antich, in using tricyclic drugs to treat children with major depression, routinely adds psychotherapy for best results. To give someone merely lithium or a tricyclic or a MAO inhibitor without some form of psychotherapy or counseling would be considered second-rate treatment. There are several reasons why.

Because of their long-standing depressive disorder, many if not most patients have not learned how to cope with their day-to-day problems. Psychotherapy helps them to do so.

Moreover, people with a major affective disorder rooted in biology often have deficiencies in their ability to relate to other people and to handle their emotions. Some have lived with this situation for ten, twenty, or thirty years—perhaps longer. Even people with a neurotic depression caused by a reaction to some life circumstance may be living with a distorted view of other people and the world, having used inefficient psychological defenses (such as denying for many years that anything in their behavior is abnormal) before seeking help. The antidepressant drug, given such people by a psychiatrist, corrects or at least puts into better order the chemical imbalance in their brain, but it does not undo all those years of suffering, of living with little control over their emotions, of maintaining an incorrect view of people and circumstances, and of using inappropriate defenses. The only way these latter issues can be approached is through psychotherapy, which may restore the emotional imbalance.

SEVEN

Guidelines to Handling Depressed Children

*S*ELDOM do we look upon the child as a small human being, struggling as most of the rest of us struggle to make sense of life, to satisfy needs, and to meet the challenges that arise. One way he differs from adults is in the terrific proportion of newness with which he must cope. Meeting for the first time the child next door, entering the wonderful and bewildering world of the supermarket, going on an airplane trip, starting nursery school or kindergarten, changing living places—all these and hundreds of other adventures may be scary or pleasant or stressful, depending mainly on the child's temperament, but also to some extent on the way that parents or other close figures have prepared him to meet such experiences.

Lois Murphy of The Menninger Foundation talks about the stress associated with moving, in her book *The Widening World of Childhood:*

For adults, moving is often going to something expected to be more gratifying—for the husband, a promotion, a better opportunity, or better salary, or better living situation, better neighborhood, better house. The child lives in a narrower world of time and space, [where] present satisfactions are real; in general, the future is vague and hard to imagine. Hopes, plans, and ideas of progress for the family may not have developed. What means most to him are his friends, familiar surroundings, his present home. It is often impossible for him to imagine feeling at home anywhere else. Unlike his father, his entire feeling may be one of going away from, of loss, separation from the beloved realities of the present with no capacity to conjure up a potentially satisfying new at-homeness. This is reinforced by the feelings of loss felt by the child's companions.

The complexity of human behavior, difficult for adults to unravel in the best of circumstances, is more so for children. In the process of realizing their potential and learning to deal with newness, they are developing—and *changing as they develop*. Lois Murphy describes this process of change as follows:

During the first four or five years of life most children are confronted with demands to accept and come to terms with numerous new situations. Some of these involve challenges to engage in new activities which may require the integration of new coordinations and skills, however well established some of the elements of these may be. Some of the skills demanded are not merely new, but difficult for the child's level of maturity and capacity. New challenges may accordingly arouse some apprehension. The effort to deal with both internal tensions and external pressures optimally evokes spontaneous, constructive efforts which are however realistically limited by the child's total resources at that point. These coping efforts are enhanced in certain children, and in other children constrained or decreased by the tension aroused by the possibility of failure.

Many parents speak of *stages* that children go through, usually meaning periods of irritating or difficult behavior. Sometimes they're right: a difficult or faddish period may indeed be a stage from which the child will safely emerge. But sometimes these parents are wrong, and they are never more wrong than when they think of a serious childhood depression as a stage or a temporary condition.

Parents may make this mistake because they have noticed that the child is continually changing; they reason that his depressive behavior may change, too. Or they may make it because they put too great a faith in the old wives' tale that children outgrow thumb sucking, bedwetting, fear of the dark, and lying, particularly if they have understanding, loving, and rather strict parents. But parents commonly fail to recognize a serious childhood depression as something that both they and the child need help in coping with. The child himself usually recognizes that something is wrong, and he or she is generally the best source of information for the person called upon to make a diagnosis.

Learning to Listen to and Talk with Your Child

Depressive and other disturbed behaviors do not simply fade out. They hang on and cause recurrent difficulties. Most often the child knows that he or she is in trouble but doesn't talk about it. You, the parent, have got to start the talking—and listen well to what the child tells you. When you suspect that something is wrong with your son or daughter—when the child is not engaging in his usual activities, when he isn't having fun with his friends, when he's moping around the house, when he's falling behind in his schoolwork—you should say something like: "Is something bothering you? Have you been feeling bad? Are you upset?" Children aged six to twelve—latency-age children—and even some younger children will tell you about it. They'll tell you how sad they are, that they've been crying, that they don't have any friends, that they're not doing well at school, that they feel bad about their whole lives. What they tell you is easy enough to listen to, if you're really interested in learning what ails your child. But it may be hard to ask about. You've got to do the asking, though, for the sake of your child's emotional health. Choose a quiet time and place—after a meal, perhaps, and in the child's favorite room—and quietly fire away.

If your depressed child is an adolescent, you may not get very good answers. Probably you will have to turn to a professional for help.

Normal Depression

As they are among adults, transient depressive reactions are very common among children. Any child will display occasional periods of sadness, loneliness, self-depreciation, tearfulness, loss of interest in his or her usual activities, and disturbances of appetite or sleep.

These short-lived episodes usually follow a specific traumatic event. Janie, for instance, had lost her favorite doll, and no amount of searching had turned it up. Robert had quarreled with his best friend. Brenda's father had promised to take her to the amusement park, but at the last minute had been called in due to an emergency at work. The transitory depressions that follow such events generally last no longer than a few days, or a week or two at most.

But there is one clear-cut exception: bereavement following the loss of a loved one, such as a parent, sibling, friend, or even a favorite pet. In such cases, symptoms of depression lasting as long as six months are considered a normal grief reaction. You should do what any normal human being does about someone who is suffering: you should be sympathetic and caring. But there is no need for clinical help.

Another cause of normal depression in children is moving. The loss of friends, neighborhood, school, and home usually sets off a mild depression that frequently lasts until the child begins to feel at home in the new environment.

So, under many circumstances, a depressive response is normal. But when the response or reaction becomes more intense, lasts longer, and, in particular, is not related to an obvious source of stress, it is time to be concerned, for a mental illness may be in the making.

Recognizing a Depressive Illness

The exact line between a normal depression and a depression that is or may become a mental illness is very difficult to draw. But there are a number of signs and symptoms that should alert parents, teachers, and doctors to the presence of a more serious disorder if they occur too long or are of at least moderate intensity.

Of all the possible danger signs, the two most important by far are these:

Dysphoric mood (The word is from the Greek for "poor attitude.") The child feels sad, blue, hopeless, low, down in the dumps, worried, and irritable.

Anhedonia (Without pleasure.) The child lacks interest or doesn't take pleasure in most usual activities, such as sports, hobbies, or interactions with friends or family.

Other signs are:

• Poor appetite and weight loss or, on the contrary, excessive eating.

• Sleep disturbances, such as insomnia, sleeplessness, nightmares, restless sleep, and early morning awakening. Excessive sleep may be an indicator, too.

• A loss of energy that shows itself in lying around the house and feeling tired, listless, fatigued.

• Psychosomatic agitation, which is apparent when the child is restless, fidgety, unable to sit still.

• Self-reproach or excessive or inappropriate guilt. The child has a tendency to blame himself for everything that goes wrong in his environment. For example, he may show guilt over school grades even though his performance has been better than average, or guilt over parental quarrels even though he had nothing to do with them.

• Diminished ability to think and concentrate. This may be observed in ordinary conversation but is more frequently seen in a drop in school performance.

• Recurrent thoughts of death or suicide, or any suicidal behavior. Such thoughts may be brought up spontaneously by the child or may be elicited gently during conversation.

Seeking Professional Help

If you suspect a depressive problem in a child, what is the best course to follow? At the beginning, we would counsel waiting. Reactive depressions, including grief reactions, are not only common but self-limiting; that is, they often improve without intervention. Also, it's worth talking with and listening to the child, to probe deeper into his world, depressive or not. However, if the symptoms noted above persist or worsen, help should be sought.

This help may be a visit to a pediatrician or a consultation with your priest, minister, rabbi, or school counselor. Having seen many children, these professionals usually can clarify and evaluate matters. They are in a good position to help you decide whether further help, particularly a consultation with a psychiatrist having a special interest in childhood depression, is needed.

How to Help at Home

While professional help is important, there are also important measures parents can take. First, avoid scapegoating when dealing with the child. Scapegoating is the tendency to single out a child and blame him for anything that goes wrong in the family's life, whether or not he is at fault. This process can be very subtle and sometimes takes utmost diligence to detect. The problem is complicated by the depressed child's tendency to accept blame.

Next, give a depressed child special amounts of attention, praise, and emotional support. The most important kind of emotional support is the personal involvement of the parents with the child. Generally speaking, the depressed child needs extra time with the parents alone. Often, other relatives—brothers, sisters, grandparents, uncles, and aunts—can be brought into the picture. Depending on circumstances, a warm involvement with other relatives can be the best form of treatment.

Finally, when losses occur, allow the child the freedom to work through his grief. In other words, allow him to end the grief by grieving. When the grieving process is ended prematurely, there may well be a depressive illness later in life. Once the grief has run its course, give the child every assistance in finding substitute persons and things to love.

In sum, often children who feel sad, blue, low, down in the dumps, or hopeless don't show their feelings to their parents. They may show them to their friends, or they may keep them to themselves. You almost always have to ask the child how he or she is feeling. There is a notable exception—irritability. When a child is feeling sad and blue, he will often display irritability, and this a parent can usually pick up. When you find your normally pleasant child irritated with his friends or by his schoolwork or by every vicissitude in his life, it's time to ask if anything is bothering him or her. Ask specifically: Have you been feeling sad or blue? The answer will often be "yes," and you'll have started the ball rolling.

Watchful parents should be able to pick up just as read- .

ily the feelings of the child who has lost pleasure in everything. Take, for example, the child whose favorite hobby is building model airplanes. Suddenly you notice that the models are just sitting around. You begin paying attention to his other activities and notice that the train set is not being played with, that the bicycle is not being ridden, and that the child is no longer having friends in or going out to meet them.

Poor appetite, another sign of depression, should be very evident. The depressed child will say he doesn't want any more, and all the pushing in the world won't get you very far.

Children won't generally tell you about sleep disturbances without being asked. But you'll notice that they're quite tired even though they seem to have been sleeping enough. Or you will hear them up early in the morning and wonder why.

A loss of energy is very clear. You'll notice the child lying around the house, with no get-up-and-go.

Psychomotor agitation, or hyperactivity, is rather rare in depressed children; but it is easy to spot when it occurs. The child may be fidgety and all over the place and you may feel you are being driven out of your mind.

When irritability occurs, there is often self-reproach. Not only will the child complain about school and just about everything else in his life, he will go on to say that it's all his fault. He feels terrible. "Why are my grades falling off? Because I'm so stupid." "Why did I have to miss that goal in the soccer game? I just wasn't giving it enough attention." "Why can't I ride my bike better? It's all my fault because I don't try hard enough." Depressed kids are down on themselves for everything.

Difficulty with thinking and concentrating, another mark of depression, is usually very hard for a parent to detect and is more likely to be picked up by a schoolteacher.

Thoughts about suicide and death are almost never mentioned spontaneously by children. But if you're worried about sadness, irritability, or self-reproach in a child, it's highly important to ask him or her about such thoughts. We have found them in half of the children we've studied.

In closing this chapter, we should like to emphasize the grieving child. He doesn't show grief the way adults do. Nor is grief internalized or made part of himself, as are other kinds of sadness in children. What you will see in the grieving child is not so much irritability or self-reproach as a tendency toward not enjoying usual activities. One of the best things to do with such children is to give them an opportunity to ventilate their feelings. Depending on the situation, say to them: "Gee, you miss Grandma as much as I do"; or "Haven't you missed Timmy since he was hit by that automobile?"; or "Isn't it sad that poor old Shep died?" Then they will talk very openly about the loss— often crying, often displaying just as much feeling as you probably have kept hidden. But, as noted earlier, you have to elicit this information from the child. Otherwise he will mope around quietly, and you will just think about your own sadness (if the loss was yours as well as his) and never know that your child was quite as sad as you.

In the next chapter we shall discuss research now being done on childhood depression and the research that needs to be done in the future before we know all that we should know about preventing, diagnosing, and treating this disorder.

EIGHT

Current and Future Explorations

*A*N IMPORTANT ADVANCE in the perception of childhood depression has been made in little more than a dozen years of study: from denial of the disorder to recognition that it not only exists but is widespread and can be successfully treated by psychotherapy and drugs in much the same fashion as the adult counterpart. However, there are many unresolved issues concerning childhood depression that further research must address. In this chapter we shall discuss some of the mysteries that researchers are trying to solve. We shall do so in two time frames. In the first, we'll consider research covering the present and the near future—research, say, that may pay off within the next few years. In the second, we'll discuss research covering the more distant future.

Research of the Present and Near Future

One vastly important and fascinating question concerns the etiology of childhood depression. Is the disorder inherited? And, if so, how often? Does it occur as a result of a trauma to the baby before or during birth, or shortly afterward? Or is it brought on by unfortunate occurrences in the child's life, perhaps years after birth?

Five years ago we and our colleague, Dr. Carolyn Zahn-Waxler, at the National Institute of Mental Health, were given a chance to throw light on such questions when we learned that seven of our adult manic-depressive patients were expecting children. Some of the patients were the prospective fathers; some, the mothers. It was a wonderful opportunity to observe these children at risk to affective illness and to follow their development.

There were seven such infants, and seven control infants of well parents, and we decided to study them when they were twelve, fifteen, and eighteen months old, each time putting them through a standardized play procedure. We videotaped the children's responses to various situations— what they did when faced with blocks and other toys; how they interacted with strangers as compared with their behavior with their mothers; how they reacted to separation from their mothers. The videotapes were then examined and analyzed in collaboration with Drs. Theodore Gaensbauer and Robert Harmon from the University of Colorado. A remarkable difference was found to exist between the two groups of children. This difference was present already at twelve months of age but was much more pronounced at eighteen months. For instance, the children with a bipolar parent showed an increasing tendency from twelve to eighteen months to be insecure in their attachment to their parents. In other words, they showed that they didn't quite trust their mothers to take care of them or at least didn't seem to be sure whether they could trust them or not. Some of the children with a depressed parent actually avoided their mothers and showed a preference for a stranger. None of the control children acted that way.

The children of bipolar parents also showed considerable difficulty in regulating their moods. Whereas the control children showed happiness and pleasure when they were playing by themselves, the children of bipolar parents showed more negative emotions: at twelve months they were fearful; at eighteen months, angry. In situations where control children tended to show pleasure in what they were doing or watching, the children of bipolar parents tended to be unhappy.

When mothers left the room, the children of well parents were more upset than the other children, but the former showed a marked capacity to recover quickly when the mothers reappeared. In contrast, the children of depressed parents were less fearful when the mothers left and seemed less glad than the others to see them when they returned.

As the children grew older, we engaged them in more complex research procedures that included observations of their behavior with their peers and families, and their reaction to other adults engaged in mock arguments or fights. The children from the bipolar families frequently showed a great deal of distress in response to conflicts and suffering of adults. They were also less able to maintain friendly relations with peers, unlike the control children. In addition, these toddlers showed disturbed behavior toward peers and adults that included excessive, displaced, or undirected aggression. These patterns of emotional disregulation, accompanied by deficiencies in social behavior, represent perhaps a prototype of depression, since they are present in depressive disorders in children at all ages.

Differences in Child-Rearing Patterns

Drs. Marian Radke-Yarrow, Carolyn Zahn-Waxler, and the authors plan to continue to look for the earliest forerunners of depression; to study how depression develops in infants, and how the parental rearing patterns or other environmental factors—in addition to hereditary ones—may contribute to depression. Finally, we hope to draw from our findings implications for how to treat predepressive states and, possibly, how to prevent them from developing into full-blown disorders.

At present, we are investigating more fully differences in the rearing practices of depressed and well mothers. Although no results from this large study are yet available, we do have some preliminary information about the children of the first twenty-seven families examined. We looked at two children from each family—a toddler aged two or three, and an older sibling aged five to eight. None of the toddlers met the criteria for psychopathology outlined in *DSM-III*. However, about one-third of them showed behavior disturbances similar to those noted by Dr. Zahn-Waxler and reported upon earlier in this chapter. Among the older siblings, seven out of seventeen of those with a depressed mother had clear diagnoses of major or minor depression. The older children of well mothers did not demonstrate such disorders.

We hope that the research results reported here will throw new light on the causes of childhood depression, will improve psychiatrists' ability to detect disorders early (before they have become full-fledged disorders), and will make it possible to give the best-informed counseling to the parents of even one-year-olds and to provide more effective counseling and other forms of therapy to both children and parents.

Current Diagnostic Research

One of the daily rhythmic functions that is disturbed in depressed children (see chapter 4) is the secretion of cortisol, a hormone produced by stress. Elva Poznanski, professor of psychiatry at the University of Illinois, has begun to investigate whether cortisol secretion patterns can be used to diagnose the presence of a major, so-called endogenous, depression that is probably of biological origin. Some of the studies of adults have shown very promising results in this area.

What Poznanski and several other investigators are doing is giving each child studied a small dose of dexamethasone in the evening. This is a drug known to suppress the secretion of cortisol. The next afternoon a blood sample is drawn and the cortisol level measured. If this level is under five micrograms per deciliter it can be assumed that the child's depression is not of the endogenous type. On the other hand, if the cortisol level is over five micrograms per deciliter the child most probably does have an endogenous depression and drug therapy should be seriously considered.

Dr. Puig-Antich has begun working along somewhat similar lines. First he identified the twenty-four-hour excretion patterns of cortisol in children with endogenous depressive disorders as similar to those in depressed adults. The total excretion is elevated, and, differing from normal children, it doesn't cease completely at any time during the twenty-four-hour cycle.

Puig-Antich's most interesting findings to date concern the secretion of growth hormone in response to a lowering of blood sugar. Normal children whose blood sugar is lowered after being given insulin show a substantial rise in the blood level of growth hormone, while children with endogenous depressive disorders fail to respond in such fashion. What is fascinating is Puig-Antich's assertion that his findings persist in these children even after their recovery, unlike all other biological changes, which usually return to normal upon recovery. If his findings are confirmed, they would constitute a stable characteristic (so-called trait marker) indicative of biological vulnerability to depression.

Research with a More Distant Payoff: Invulnerability

In studies we are conducting on invulnerable children, with Dr. David Pellegrini from Catholic University, we ask the question: why do some children, born of at least one depressed parent and brought up in a household where that parent's depressed behavior could be expected to affect all other members, escape becoming depressed themselves? What makes them invulnerable? Even assuming that they have not inherited the gene or genes that predispose one to the disorder, how have they escaped important environmental factors—including the closeness of a depressed parent, with his or her depressive way of interpreting life? The answers to these puzzling questions would improve our ability to prevent the development of depression.

New Work in Genetics

A recombinant DNA laboratory has recently been installed in the department of psychogeneticist Dr. Elliot Gershon at the National Institute of Mental Health. DNA stands for deoxyribonucleic acid, the stuff of which genes are made. "Recombinant" signifies that one will be able to combine a section of one gene with another section of the same gene or with a different gene; by studying how the altered gene operates in the organism into which it has been introduced, one will be able to deduce which gene segments are responsible for what operations. Gershon and his associates will be looking primarily for the gene or genes that transmit manic-depressive illness. He hopes that stable chemical characteristics of this gene will be found attached to white blood cells or cells in other tissues. If such a characteristic can be identified, tests to determine its presence can presumably be developed. Then several highly important avenues will open up to clinical practitioners and researchers. For one thing, they will be able to test children for the presence of the genetic defect by testing for the characteristic that would be a genetic marker, or an indicator of the presence of the gene or genes responsible for affective illness. Then, it is hoped, through education of the child and his family, one may be able to minimize the possibility that this defect will be expressed as an affective disorder. In addition, one will be able to look at infants, toddlers, and older children and perhaps separate the effect of the genetic from the psychological factors causing affective disorders. New drugs and new approaches to psychotherapy might well result.

The importance of genetic markers can readily be seen in such a disease as phenylketonuria (PKU)—a disorder in which the child appears normal at birth but lacks the enzyme to break down one of the amino acids in dietary proteins, phenylalanine. In PKU, phenylalanine builds up in the blood and causes brain damage, quickly leading to mental retardation, which may become profound. The missing enzyme is the genetic marker. Its absence can be readily detected through a test given in infancy, the earlier the better. If the enzyme is missing, the infant is placed on a phenylalanine-free diet, and retardation may be prevented, or at least ameliorated.

Depression Viewed as Learned Helplessness

Odd though it may seem, experiments performed with mongrel dogs fifteen years ago are leading to a new idea about the nature and treatment of childhood depression. The principal researcher is Dr. Martin E. P. Seligman of the University of Pennsylvania. In 1967, Seligman and co-workers exposed dogs to uncontrollable electric shocks. Then they put each animal in a two-compartment cage, where the shocks could be controlled. All the animal had to do when shock was applied was to jump from one compartment to the other. In the second compartment he was safe. But most dogs, probably because of their previous inability to escape the shocks, just lay passively and took shock after shock without a whimper. They failed to learn how they could escape by simply jumping over a low barrier. The researchers described the dogs' attitude as *learned helplessness.* The animals had learned, during the first phase of the experiment, that nothing they could do would put an end to their misery. When conditions were changed so that they could do something, the initial lesson remained and they made no attempt to escape.

Seligman has since argued that there are strikingly similar parallels between helplessness and depression. He proposes that the inability to control a bad situation or event leads some people to an expectation of helplessness and that this expectation leads to odd or abnormal behavior and eventually to depression. But the extent of such behavior depends upon the "causal attributions" people make about the uncontrollable events—in other words, how they account for the causes of the events that trouble them.

Does an individual believe that the uncontrollable events are caused by something within himself, by his own characteristics? In other words, does he think that he himself is responsible? In that case, the causal attribution—or the reason the person gives for a bad event—is described as *internal.* If the individual attributes the uncontrollable events to factors that persist over time, the attribution is described as *stable.* Finally, if the individual attributes the uncontrollable events to causes present in a variety of situations, not in just one or two, the attribution is described as *global.* According to Seligman,

> To the degree that a person points to internal, stable, and global causes of bad events, then that person is increasingly likely to be helpless and depressed once a bad event is encountered. Depression (in children and adults) results from characteristics of an individual (i.e., the "depressive" attributional style) in conjunction with characteristics of the environment (i.e., uncontrollable bad events). Neither the attributional style nor the uncontrollable events alone result in widespread helplessness and depression; only their co-occurrence leads to depression.*

How does a child acquire his attributional style, or the characteristic way he or she explains events that markedly affect his or her life? Seligman attempted to throw light on this question by comparing the styles of eighty parents with those of their offspring. He found that a mother's attributional style for bad events correlated with her child's attributional style for bad events and with her child's depressive symptoms. The father's attributional style, however, was not related to the styles of his children or of his mate, apparently because much of his life was lived separately. "The child may learn attributional style (or depressive symptoms) from its mother," Seligman speculates, "and then the depressions of mother and child may maintain each other . . ."

If a maladaptive attributional style leads to depression, can the style be changed? As a major part of his continuing research, Seligman has demonstrated that it can. In a preliminary study, his subjects were twenty depressed children who believed that bad events in their life were caused

---

*Seligman and Peterson, 1982.

by their own behavior. Seligman tried to help these children to see that they did not have to blame themselves and that a bad situation need not endure but can often be changed—in short, that their thinking was fallacious regarding the causes of their disorder. Seligman reported that, with his treatment methods, some 80 percent of these depressed children improved remarkably, and that their improvement has continued through the first six months he has followed them.

Some Recent Biological Studies on Adult Affective Disorders

Since affective disorders in adults may, in some cases, have their beginnings in childhood, a brief account of some of the new research in adult affective illness may be pertinent.

Abnormality in chemical transmission • As noted earlier, the study of chemicals that help transmit messages from one nerve cell to another in the brain has provided fruitful information for helping to understand how brain chemistry is related to affective disorders. Such information is essential to understanding the mechanism and action of antidepressant medications crucial to the development of more refined and effective drugs.

Man's own morphine—another neurotransmitter • The treatment of affective disorders may eventually be enhanced, too, through research on man's own made-in-the-brain morphine. Two pioneers in this field include Dr. Candice Pert of NIMH, who, with Dr. Solomon Snyder of Johns Hopkins, has studied the compound *endorphin*, a name made up of two words meaning "the morphine within." Several endorphins closely related to morphine are known. One, called beta-endorphin, has been found to be effective in treating some cases of depression. Drug companies are making synthetic analogues of the most potent of these compounds, and in experiments with animals, one of these has turned out to be a hundred times stronger than morphine.

How do we know that morphinelike compounds exist in the brain? A suggestive answer comes from the old observation that schizophrenics seem to be much less sensitive than normal persons to pain and discomfort. In a recent experiment, NIMH scientists studied a number of hospitalized schizophrenic patients and found that on the average they were indeed less bothered by pain than normal people. A few of the patients were given opium antagonists—compounds that block the effects of opiates (a class of drugs, of which morphine is one) and are used in the treatment of opiate addiction, on the assumption that if a person no longer gets pleasure from taking a drug he will stop using it—and their sensitivity to pain increased considerably. Apparently the antagonists can block not only the pain-killing effects of synthetic morphine but those of endorphins.

So what could be the endorphins' role in affective disorders? At present, investigators are considering two possibilities. Maybe they prevent or correct depressed feelings; or perhaps they are responsible for our good feelings when we experience joy or happiness—in which case they would be part of the brain's so-called reward system. At any rate, endorphins continue to be studied by Dr. Frederick K. Goodwin, director of NIMH's Intramural Research Program, his colleagues, and other investigators. The definitive answers are not yet available and it may be some years before we know how man's own morphine can help in treating mental illness.

Biological rhythms • Many functions of the body have a twenty-four-hour, or circadian, rhythm. Sleeping and waking follow such a rhythm. So does body temperature. Others include REM periods; the appearance of breakdown products of the neurotransmitters in the body's fluids; and the secretion of many hormones. Goodwin and Thomas A. Wehr, also of the NIMH, are studying abnormalities in such rhythms. During periods of depression, they have found, most of the rhythms are shifted considerably. Thus they have some evidence to back their belief that abnormal rhythms contribute to major depression.

If that is the case, is there any way of bringing the rhythms back to normal? Goodwin and Wehr tried to do so in a manic-depressive woman by having her go to sleep six hours earlier than usual. In each of two trials, the patient had a complete remission lasting about two weeks. But she then became depressed again, presumably because the other rhythmic functions didn't keep pace with the new sleep-waking rhythm and gradually returned to the pattern characteristic of her depression.

Vasopressin and learning • In another research study, Goodwin and associates at NIMH used an analogue of vasopressin (a hormone, found in brain areas concerned with memory and learning, which seems to work by affecting the brain's reward system) to treat depression. The analogue, called desamide desanginine vasopressin (DDAVP), works like vasopressin. It seems to make a person feel better if he succeeds in learning or memorizing something. Because of this effect, Goodwin began investigating vasopressin's effect in depressed people who often feel hopeless and worthless. In the depressive stage of an affective disorder, they found, only low levels of vasopressin breakdown products appear in the spinal fluid, an indication that less than normal amounts of the compound itself are present in the brain or at least that it functions poorly. But in the hypomanic stage of the disorder, the levels of vasopressin were found to be higher, and memory and learning functions were better than average.

The investigators concluded from these findings that it might be helpful to somehow increase the level of vasopressin in depressed persons. As the supply of vasopressin, which is extracted from the brains of animals, is extremely limited, and as no way is yet known of making the compound in the laboratory, the Goodwin team used the synthetic analogue with depressed persons who had failed to respond to other drugs. The results were very exciting. Measured by their ability to recall words given in categories (words relating to furniture, for example, or to clothing, people, ornaments, and so on), the memory of the six patients in whom the drug was tried returned to normal or above. "It's like I got my brain back," said one patient. Dutch scientists are now experimenting with a new and possibly more potent analogue of vasopressin, desglycinamide anginine vasopressin (DGAVP).

Summary

Research to date indicates that children of depressed parents or grandparents are much more likely to become depressed than children with no depressed close relatives. The rate of the disorder among the latter children is about 5 to 10 percent, while in the group with a family history of depression it may be 30 to 50 percent. This increase is cause for keeping a close watch on the vulnerable—or at-risk—children. Some may have inherited a predisposition to the illness, while others may have acquired the illness through environmental exposure to a depressed adult who serves as a role model, particularly if the adult's depression is chronic.

A study begun by us and our colleagues indicates that even as infants the children of manic-depressive parents differ in a number of ways from children of well parents. They show an increasing tendency, from twelve to eighteen months of age, to be insecure in their attachment to their mothers; are more likely to have problems with eating and sleeping; show more negative reactions while playing; are more tense and more likely to engage in aggressive behavior without apparent cause. These children continue to be followed. In addition, a larger study, of differences in the rearing practices of well and depressed mothers, is in progress in our department at NIMH.

The improvement of diagnosis is also under study. The criteria used with adults can usually be applied in diagnosing major depressive disorders in children. But in many depressed children the symptoms of the disorder appear to be much less severe than in adults. It is still not completely clear to what extent these symptoms foretell a major disorder in adolescence and adult life. The study of the natural history of childhood depression should help answer this important question.

Another question impelling researchers is how to identify those children who are genetically vulnerable to depression. Means of identifying such children early may make it possible to take action that will prevent the development of the disorder.

Research with a more distant payoff offers many fascinating possibilities. The following are among the subjects on which investigators are presently working:

Most children of a severely depressed parent, who may be genetically vulnerable to the disorder and / or were exposed to a depressed parent's attitudes and behavior, do not become depressed. What factors make them apparently invulnerable?

Assuming there are one or more genes responsible for a predisposition to depression, what is their nature and how can their pres-

ence be detected? An answer to these questions could help us identify children likely to develop the disorder and take protective steps.

What effect does the environment—in particular, the rearing practices of depressed parents—have on the development of depression in children?

Experimentally induced learned helplessness in animals seems to provide a suitable model for the thinking of depressed children, i.e., the connection of their inability to control their life circumstances. Work continues to clarify fully how a child develops learned helplessness and how this state is related to parental attitudes.

More information is being sought on how depression is affected by, or affects, the body's circadian, or twenty-four-hour, rhythms. These include sleeping, waking, body temperature, and the output of several hormones. In some adult depressions, many of the rhythms may play an important role in the causation of major adult depression. It is possible that their correction may cure or at least alleviate such a disorder.

Among the new drugs tested for their usefulness against depression are an analogue of vasopressin, a naturally occurring brain chemical that seems to improve the memory and sometimes alleviate the depression itself; and the endorphins, made-in-the-brain compounds very much like morphine.

Though it may be years before the full story of depression—its causes, prevention, and treatment—is known, vigorous research under way in all the areas mentioned in this summary and in many others is likely to continue until the mystery of this most common mental disorder is finally solved.

Epilogue

THE OUTLOOK for depressed children is generally good. Despite the relatively high frequency of depression, particularly in children of manic-depressive parents, it appears that probably only a minority of children have a genetic disorder and thus are at great risk for future illness.

Regardless of cause, depressed children as a group are very responsive to a variety of treatments, both pharmacological and psychological. Even children with severe depression who required hospitalization have often been found years later to be well adjusted and functioning well.

Improvement has been pronounced in less disturbed children seen and followed in our clinic. Not only have children responded well to psychotherapy with or without medication, but in many instances dramatic improvement has occurred spontaneously without formal treatment. We attribute this spontaneous improvement to several factors. First, contact with the clinic, however brief, often acts as a catalyst to positive change in the family—in particular, a healthier attitude toward the depressed child. Second, the child's normal maturational push for growth often helps him or her overcome the disorder. Despite such occasional spontaneous cures, we recommend that treatment be undertaken in all cases in which a clear-cut diagnosis of childhood depression is made, in order to ensure a favorable outcome rather than leave things up to chance.

In closing we should like to emphasize two points:

Early detection and treatment of depressed children, before the depression becomes a way of life, is essential. The intensity of treatment will depend on the severity of the child's illness and the degree of the family's psychological health.

Given timely and appropriate help, most depressed children can be helped to live a normal and productive life.

References

Abraham, K. Notes on the psychoanalytic investigation and treatment of manic-depressive insanity and allied conditions. In *Selected Papers on Psychoanalysis*. London: Hogarth Press and Institute of Psychoanalysis, 1927.

Abraham, K. The first pregenital stage of libido. In *Selected Papers on Psychoanalysis*. London: Hogarth Press and Institute of Psychoanalysis, 1927.

Abraham, K. A short study of the development of the libido, viewed in the light of mental disorders. In *Selected Papers on Psychoanalysis*. London: Hogarth Press and Institute of Psychoanalysis, 1927.

Ajuriaguerra, J. D. *Manuel de Psychiatrie de L'Enfant*. Paris: Masson, 1971.

Alexander, F., and French, T. *Psychoanalytic Therapy: Principles and Applications*. New York: Ronald Press, 1946.

Allen, F. H. *Psychotherapy With Children*. New York: W. W. Norton, 1942.

Annell, A. L. Lithium in the treatment of children and adolescents. *Acta Psychiatrica Scandinavica*, 1969, *207*, 19.

Annell, A. L. Manic-depressive illness in children and effect of treatment with lithium carbonate. *Acta Paedopsychiatrica*, 1969, *39*, 292.

Annell, A. L. *Depressive States in Childhood and Adolescence*. Stockholm: Almquist & Wiksell, 1972.

Anthony, E. J. Primary prevention with schoolchildren. In H. H. Barten and L. Bellak (eds.). *Progress in Community Mental Health*, vol. 2. New York: Grune & Stratton, 1972.

Anthony, E. J. Psychoneurotic disorders. In A. M. Freedman and H. G. Kaplan (eds.). *Comprehensive Textbook of Psychiatry*. Baltimore: Williams & Wilkins, 1975.

Anthony, E. J. Childhood depression. In E. J. Anthony and T. Benedek (eds.). *Depression and Human Existence*. Boston: Little, Brown & Co., 1975.

Anthony, E. J. The influence of a manic-depressive environment on the developing child. In E. J. Anthony and T. Benedek (eds.). *Depression and Human Existence*. Boston: Little, Brown & Co., 1975.

Anthony, E. J., and Scott, P. Manic-depressive psychosis in childhood. *Journal of Child Psychology and Psychiatry*, 1960, *1*, 53.

Apter, A., Borengasser, M. A.; Hamovit, J.; Bartko, J. J.; Cytryn, L.; McKnew, D. H. A four-year follow-up of depressed children. *Journal of Preventive Psychiatry*, 1982, *1*, 89.

Beck, A. T. Depressive neurosis. In *American Handbook of Psychiatry*, vol. 3. New York: Basic Books, 1974.

Beck, A. T., and Beamesderfer, A. Assessment of depression: the depression inventory. In P. Pichot (ed.). *Psychological Measurements in Psychopharmacology: Modern Problems in Pharmacopsychiatry.* Basel: Karger, 1974.

Bell, N. W., and Vogel, E. F. The emotionally disturbed child as the family scapegoat. In N. W. Bell and E. F. Vogel (eds.). *The Family.* Glencoe, Ill.: Free Press, 1960.

Bellak, L. *Manic-depressive Psychosis and Allied Conditions.* New York: Grune & Stratton, 1952.

Bibring, E. The mechanism of depression. In P. Greenacre (ed.). *Affective Disorders.* New York: International Universities Press, 1953.

Bibring, E. The development and problems of the theory of instincts. *International Journal of Psychoanalysis*, 1969, *22*, 102.

Bierman, J., Silverstein, A., and Finesinger, J. A depression in a six-year old boy with acute poliomyelitis. *Psychoanalytic Study of the Child*, 1958, *13*, 430.

Bleuler, E. *Dementia Praecox or the Group of Schizophrenias.* New York: International Universities Press, 1950.

Bowlby, J. Separation anxiety. *International Journal of Psychoanalysis*, 1960, *41*, 89.

Bowlby, J. Grief and mourning in infancy and early childhood. *Psychoanalytic Study of the Child*, 1960, *15*, 9.

Bowlby, J. Separation anxiety: a critical review of the literature. *Journal of Child Psychology and Psychiatry*, 1961, *1*, 251.

Bowlby, J. Process of mourning. *International Journal of Psychoanalysis*, 1961, *42*, 317.

Bowlby, J. Pathological mourning and childhood mourning. *Journal of American Psychoanalytic Association*, 1963, *11*, 500.

Bowlby, J. *Attachment and Loss, I: Attachment.* New York: Basic Books, 1969.

Bowlby, J. *Attachment and Loss, II: Separation.* New York: Basic Books, 1973.

Brown, F. Childhood bereavement and subsequent psychiatric disorder. *British Journal of Psychiatry*, 1966, *112*, 1035.

Brumback, R. A., and Weinberg, W. A. Mania in childhood II. *Archives of American Journal of Diseases of Children*, 1977, *131*, 1122.

Campbell, J. D. Manic-depressive psychosis in children. *Journal of Nervous and Mental Disorders*, 1952, *166*, 424.

Conners, C. K. Child psychiatry: organic therapies. In A. M. Freedman, H. I. Kaplan, and B. J. Sadock (eds.). *Comprehensive Textbook of Psychiatry II.* Baltimore: Williams & Wilkins, 1975.

Coppen, A.; Shaw, D. M.; Malleson, A.; Eccleston, E.; and Grundy, G. Tryptomine metabolism in depression. *British Journal of Psychiatry*, 1965, *111*, 993.

Cytryn, L. Discussion of childhood depression. In J. G. Schultenbrandt and A. Raskin (eds.). *Depression in Childhood.* New York: Raven Press, 1977.

Cytryn, L., and McKnew, D. H. Proposed classification of childhood depression. *American Journal of Psychiatry*, 1972, *129*, 149.

Cytryn, L., and McKnew, D. H. Proposed classification of childhood depression. In S. Chess and A. Thomas (eds.). *Annual Progress in Child Psychiatry and Child Development.* New York: Bruner/Mazel, 1973.

Cytryn, L., and McKnew, D. H. Biochemical correlates of affective disorders in children. *Archives of General Psychiatry*, 1974, *31*, 659.

Cytryn, L., and McKnew, D. H. Factors influencing the changing clinical expression of the depressive process in children. *American Journal of Psychiatry*, 1974, *131*, 879.

Cytryn, L., and McKnew, D. H. Factors influencing the changing clinical expression of the depressive process in children. In S. Chess and A. Thomas (eds.). *Annual Progress in Child Psychiatry and Child Development*. Baltimore: Williams & Wilkins, 1975.

Cytryn, L., and McKnew, D. H. Affective disorders of childhood. In J. Nospitz (ed.). *Basic Handbook of Child Psychiatry*. New York: Basic Books, 1979.

Cytryn, L., and McKnew, D. H. Diagnosis of depression in children: reassessment. *American Journal of Psychiatry*, 1980, *137*, 22.

Cytryn, L, and McKnew, D. H. Affective disorders in childhood. In H. I. Kaplan, A. M. Friedman, and B. H. Sadock (eds.). *Comprehensive Textbook of Psychiatry*. Baltimore: Williams & Wilkins, 1980.

Cytryn, L., and McKnew, D. H. Detection and prevention of childhood depression. In E. Corfman (ed.). *NIMH Science Monographs 1*. Washington: Government Printing Office, 1980.

Cytryn, L., and McKnew, D. H. Diagnosis of depression in children: a reassessment. In S. Chess and A. Thomas (eds.). *Annual Progress in Child Psychiatry and Child Development*. New York: Bruner/Mazel, 1982.

Cytryn, L., and McKnew, D. H. Childhood depression: diagnosis and treatment. *Medicine et Hygiene*, 1982, 2359.

Cytryn, L., and McKnew, D. H. *Developmental Issues in Risk Research: The Offspring of Affectively Ill Parents*. Paper presented at the Social Science Research Council conference on "Depressive Feelings and Disorders," Philadelphia, April 1982.

Cytryn, L.; McKnew, D. H.; Bartko, J. J.; Lamour, M.; and Hamovit, J. Offspring of patients with affective disorders, II. *Journal of American Academy of Child Psychiatry*, 1982, *21*, 389.

Cytryn, L.; McKnew, D. H.; and Lamour, M. *Affective Disturbances in the Offspring of Affectively Disturbed Parents—A Developmental View*. Paper presented at the 10th Congress of the International Association for Child and Adolescent Psychiatry, Dublin, Ireland, July 1982.

Cytryn, L.; McKnew, D. H., Logue, M., and Desai, R. B. Biochemical correlates of affective disorders. *Archives of General Psychiatry*, 1974, *31*, 659.

DeNegri, M., and Moretti, M. G. Quelques aspects des depressions infantiles. *Acta Paedopsychiatrica*, 1971, *38*, 182.

Diagnostic and Statistical Manual of Mental Disorders, Third Edition (DSM-III). Washington, D.C.: American Psychiatric Association, 1978.

Dizmang, L. H. Loss, bereavement and depression in childhood. *International Psychiatry Clinic*, 1969, *6*, 175.

Durell, J., and Schildkraut, J. J. Biochemical studies of the schizophrenic and affective disorders. In S. Arietti (ed.). *American Handbook of Psychiatry*. New York: Basic Books, 1966.

Dyson, W. L., and Barcai, A. Treatment of children of lithium-responding parents. *Current Therapy and Research*, 1970, *12*, 286.

Ebert, M. H., and Kopin, I. J. Differential labeling of origins of urinary catecholamine metabolites by dopamine–C^{14}. *Transactions of the Association of American Physicians*, 1975, *28*, 256.

Ebert, M. H., Post, R. M., and Goodwin, F. K. The effect of physical activity on urinary MHPG excretion in depressed patients. *Lancet*, 1972, *2*, 766.

Engel, G. L. Anxiety and depression withdrawal: the primary affects of unpleasure. *International Journal of Psychoanalysis*, 1962, *43*, 89.

Engel, G. L., and Reichsman, F. Spontaneous and experimentally induced depression in an infant with gastric fistula. *Journal of the American Psychoanalytic Association*, 1956, *4*, 428.

Ewalt, J. R., and Farnsworth, D. L. *Textbook of Psychiatry*. New York: McGraw-Hill, 1963.

Feighner, J. P.; Robins, E.; Guze, S. B.; Woodruff, R. A.; Winokur, G.; and

Munoz, R. Diagnostic criteria for use in psychiatric research. *Archives of General Psychiatry*, 1972, *26*, 57.

Feinstein, S. C. Adolescent depression. In E. J. Anthony and T. Benedek (eds.). *Depression and Human Existence.* Boston: Little, Brown & Co., 1975.

Fish, B. Drug use in psychiatric disorders of children. *American Journal of Psychiatry*, 1968, *124*, 31.

Freud A. Introduction to the Technique of Child Analysis. *Nervous and Mental Disease Monograph*, 1929, *48*.

Freud, A. *The Ego and the Mechanisms of Defense.* New York: International Universities Press, 1946.

Freud, A. *Normality and Pathology in Childhood.* New York: International Universities Press, 1965.

Freud, S. 1915. Mourning and melancholia. In The Complete Psychological Works, The Standard Edition, vol. 14, ed. and tr. by J. Strachey. New York: W. W. Norton, 1976.

Freud, S., 1914. On narcissism: an introduction. In The Complete Psychological Works, The Standard Edition, vol. 14, ed. and tr. by J. Strachey. New York: W. W. Norton, 1976.

Freud, S., 1915. Instincts and their vicissitudes. In The Complete Psychological Works, The Standard Edition, vol. 14, ed. and tr. by J. Strachey. New York: W. W. Norton, 1976.

Freud, S., An outline of psychoanalysis (rev.) tr. by J. Strachey. New York: W. W. Norton, 1970.

Frommer, E. A. Treatment of childhood depression with antidepressant drugs. *British Medical Journal*, 1967, *1*, 729.

Frommer, E. A. Depressive illness in childhood. In A. Coppen and Walk (eds.). *Recent Developments in Affective Disorders: A Symposium.* Ashford: Headley Bros., 1968.

Garmezy, N. Children at risk: the search for the antecedents of schizophrenia, part 1. *Schizophrenia Bulletin*, 1974, *8*.

Garmezy, N. Children at risk: the search for the antecedents of schizophrenia, part 2. *Schizophrenia Bulletin*, 1974, *9*.

Gershon, E. S.; Bunney, W. E., Jr.; Leckman, J. F.; van Eerdewech, M.; and DeBauche, B. A. The inheritance of affective disorders: a review of data and of hypotheses. *Behavioral Genetics*, 1976, *6*, 227.

Gillespie, R. D. The clinical differentiation of types of depression. *Guy's Hospital Reports*, 1930, *79*, 306.

Gittlemen-Klein, R. Definitional and methodological issues concerning depressive illness in children. In J. G. Schultenbrandt and A. Raskin (eds.). *Depression in Childhood.* New York: Raven Press, 1977.

Gittelman-Klein, R., and Klein, D. F. Controlled imipramine treatment of school phobia. *Archives of General Psychiatry*, 1971, *25*, 204.

Gittelman-Klein, R., and Klein, D. F. School phobia: diagnostic considerations in the light of imipramine effects. In *Progress in Psychiatric Drug Treatment.* New York: Brunner/Mazel, 1975.

Goode, D. J.; Dekirmenjian, H.; Meltzer, H. Y.; and Maas, J. W. Relation of exercise to MHPG excretion in normal subjects. *Archives of General Psychiatry*, 1973, *29*, 391.

Greenberg, L. M., and Yellin, A. M. Blood pressure and pulse changes in hyperactive children treated with imipramine and methylphenidate. *American Journal of Psychiatry*, 1975, *132*, 1325.

Greenhill, L. L.; Rieder, R. O.; Wender, P. H.; Bucksbaum, M.; and Zahn, T. Lithium carbonate in the treatment of hyperactive children. *Archives of General Psychiatry*, 1973, *28*, 636.

Group for the Advancement of Psychiatry. *Psychopathological Disorders in Childhood.* New York: GAP, Report 62, 1966.

Hall, M. B. Our present knowledge about manic-depressive states in childhood. *Nervous Child*, 1952, *9*, 319.

Harlow, H. F., and Suomi, S. J. The nature of love—simplified. *American Psychologist*, 1970, *25*, 161.

Hinde, R. A. *Animal Behavior: A Synthesis of Ethology and Comparative Psychology.* New York: McGraw-Hill, 1970.

Hodges, K.; Kline, J.; McKnew, D. H.; Cytryn, L. The child assessment schedule: a diagnostic interview for research and clinical use. *Catalogue of Selected Documents in Psychology*, 1981, *11*, 56.

Hodges, K.; Kline, J.; Stern, L.; McKnew, D. H.; and Cytryn, L. The development of a child assessment interview for research and clinical use. *Journal of Abnormal Child Psychology*, 1982, *10*, 173.

Hodges, K.; Kline, J.; Stern, L.; Cytryn, L.; and McKnew, D. H. The CAS interview for children: a report on reliability and validity. *Journal of the American Academy of Child Psychiatry*, 1982, *21*.

Hollister, L. E.; Davis, K. L.; Overall, J. E.; and Anderson, T. Excretion of MHPG in normal subjects. *Archives of General Psychiatry*, 1978, *35*, 1410.

Jacobs, J. *Adolescent Suicide.* New York: John Wiley & Sons, Inc., 1971.

Jacobson, E. The effect of disappointment on ego and superego formation in normal and depressive development. *Psychoanalytic Review*, 1946, *33*, 129.

Jacobson, E. Contribution to the metapsychology of cyclothymic depression. In P. Greenacre (ed.). *Affective Disorders.* New York: International Universities Press, 1953.

Jacobson, E. The self and the object world: vicissitudes of their infantile cathexes and their influences on ideation and affective development. *Psychoanalytic Study of the Child*, 1954, *9*, 75.

Jacobson, E. On normal and pathological moods. *Psychoanalytic Study of the Child*, 1957, *12*, 73.

Jacobson, E. *The Self and the Object World.* New York: International Universities Press, 1964.

Jacobson, E. *Depression.* New York: International Universities Press, 1971.

Jacobson, E. The depressive personality. *International Journal of Psychiatry*, 1973, *11*, 218.

Jimerson, D. C.; Gordon, E. K.; Post, R. M.; and Goodwin, F. K. Central noradrenergic function in man: vanillylmandelic acid in CSF. *Brain Research*, 1975, *99*, 434.

Kanner, L. *Child Psychiatry.* Springfield, Ill.: Charles C. Thomas, 1947.

Kashani, J.; Husain, A.; Shekim, W. O.; Hodges, K.; Cytryn, L.; and McKnew, D. H. Current perspectives on childhood depression: an overview. *American Journal of Psychiatry*, 1981, *138*, 143.

Kashani, J.; Manning, G.; McKnew, D. H.; Cytryn, L.; Husain, A.; and Wooderson, P. Depression among incarcerated delinquents. *Psychiatry Research*, 1980, *3*, 185.

Kashani, J. H.; Silva, P. A.; Anderson, J. C.; Clarkson, S. E.; McGee, R. O.; Walton, L. A.; Williams, S. M.; Robins, A. J.; Cytryn, L.; and McKnew, D. H. The nature and prevalence of major and minor depression in a sample of nine-year-old children. *Archives of General Psychiatry*, in press.

Kaufman, I. C., and Rosenblum, L. A. Depression in infant monkeys separated from their mothers. *Science*, 1967, *155*, 1030.

Klein, D. F. Drug therapy as a means of syndromal identification and nosological revision. In J. O. Cole (ed.). *Psychopathology and Psychopharmacology.* Baltimore: Johns Hopkins University Press, 1973.

Klein, M. *The Psychoanalysis of Children*. London: Hogarth Press and Institute of Psychoanalysis, 1932.

Klein, M. A contribution to the psychogenesis of manic-depressive states. In M. Klein (ed.). *Contributions to Psychoanalysis*. London: Hogarth Press, 1948.

Klein, M. Mourning and its relation to manic-depressive states. In M. Klein (ed.). *Contributions to Psychoanalysis*. London: Hogarth Press, 1948.

Klerman, G. L. Clinical research in depression. *Archives of General Psychiatry*, 1971, *24*, 305.

Kline, N. S. *From Sad to Glad*. New York: Ballantine Books. 1974.

Kohler, C., and Beruard, F. Les etats depressifs chez l'enfant. In A. L. Annell (ed.). *Depressive States in Childhood and Adolescence*. Stockholm: Almquist & Wiksell, 1971.

Kovacs, M., and Beck, A. T. An empirical-clinical approach toward a definition of childhood depression. In J. G. Schultenbrandt and A. Raskin (eds.). *Depression in Childhood*. New York: Raven Press, 1977.

Kraepelin, E. *Clinical Psychiatry*. New York: Macmillan. 1902.

Kraepelin, E. *Psychiatrie: Ein Lehrbuch fur Studiende und Artze, II: Klinische Psychiatrie*. Leipzig: Barch, 1918.

Kuhn, R. Uber kindliche depressionen und ihre behandlung. *Schweizerische Medizinische Wochenschrift*, 1963, *93*, 86.

Kuhn, V., and Kuhn, R. Drug therapy for depression in children. Indication and methods. In A. L. Annell (ed.). *Depressive States in Childhood and Adolescence*. Stockholm: Almquist & Wiksell, 1971.

Kupfer, D. J.; Coble, P.; Kane, Y.; Petti, T.; and Conners, C. K. Imipramine and EEG sleep in children with depressive symptom. *Psychopharmacology*, 1970, *60*, 117.

Lebovici, S. Contribution psychoanalytique a la connaissance de la depression chez l'enfant. In A. L. Annell (ed.). *Depressive States in Childhood and Adolescence*. Stockholm: Almquist & Wiksell, 1971.

Leckman, J. F.; Gershon, E. S.; Nichols, A. S.; and Murphy, D. L. Reduced MAO activity in first-degree relatives of individuals with bipolar affective disorders. *Archives of General Psychiatry*, 1977, *34*, 601.

Lehmann, H. E. Psychiatric concepts of depression: nomenclature and classification. *Canadian Psychiatric Association Journal*, 1959, *4*, 1.

Leonhard, K. *Aufteilung der Endogenen Psychosen*. Berlin: Akademic Verlag, 1957.

Levy, D. Release therapy. *American Journal of Othopsychiatry*, 1939, *9*, 713.

Lewis, J. K.; McKinney, W. T., Jr.; Young, L. D.; and Kreamer, G. W. Mother-infant separation in rhesus monkeys as a model of human depression. *Archives of General Psychiatry*, 1976, *33*, 699.

Lieberman, D. Suicide among adolescents. In K. Wolff (ed.). *Patterns of Self-Destruction: Depression and Suicide*. Springfield, Ill.: Charles C. Thomas, 1970.

Lucas, A. R. Treatment of depressive states. In J. M. Wiener (ed.). *Psychopharmacology in Childhood and Adolescence*. New York: Basic Books, 1977.

Lucas, A. R.; Lockett, H. J.; and Grimm, F. Amitriptyline in childhood depression. *Disorders of the Nervous System*, 1965, *26*, 105.

Maas, J. W.; Dekirmenjian, H.; and Fawcett, J. Catecholamine metabolism, depression and stress. *Nature*, 1971 *230*, 330.

Maas, J. W.; Fawcett, J.; and Dekirmenjian, H. 3-methoxy-4-hydroxy-phenylglycol (MHPG) excretion in depressive states. *Archives of General Psychiatry*, 1968, *19*, 129.

Maas, J. W., and Landis, D. H. In vivo studies of the metabolism of norepinephrine in the central nervous system. *Journal of Pharmacological Experimental Therapy*, 1968, *163*, 147.

Mahler, M. S. On sadness and grief in infancy and childhood— loss and restoration of the symbiotic love object. *Psychoanalytic Study of the Child*, 1961, *16*, 332.

Mahler, M. S. Notes on the development of basic moods: the depressive affect. In R. M. Loewensten, L. M., Newman, M. Schur, and A. J. Solnit (eds.). *Psychoanalysis— A General Psychology*. New York: International Universities Press, 1966.

Makita, K. The rarity of "depression" in childhood. *Acta Psychiatrica Scandinavica*, 1973, *40*, 37.

Malmquist, C. P. Depressions in childhood and adolescence. I. *New England Journal of Medicine*, 1971, *284*, 887.

Malmquist, C. P. Depressions in childhood and adolescence. II. *New England Journal of Medicine*, 1971, *284*, 955.

Malmquist, C. P. Depressive phenomena in children. In B. B. Wolman (ed.). *Manual of Child psychopathology*. New York: McGraw-Hill, 1972.

McConville, B. J.; Boag, L. C.; and Purohit, A. P. Three types of childhood depression. *Canadian Psychiatric Association Journal*, 1973, *18*, 133.

McHarg, J. F. Mania in childhood. *Archives of Neurological Psychiatry*, 1954, *72*, 531.

McKinney, W. T., Jr. Behavioral models of depression in monkeys. In I. Hanin and E. Usdin (eds.). *Animal Models in Psychiatry*. Oxford: Pergamon Press, 1977.

McKnew, D. H. Use of psychotropic medication in adolescent psychiatry. In J. Novello (ed.). *A Short Course in Adolescent Psychiatry*. New York: Bruner / Mazel, 1979.

McKnew, D. H. *Discussion of "Suicide in Children and the Family."* Paper presented at the Annual Meeting of the American Psychiatric Association, Toronto, May 1982.

McKnew, D. H., and Cytryn, L. Changes in urinary metabolites in affective disorders in children. *Pediatric Research*, 1972, *6*, 425.

McKnew, D. H., and Cytryn, L. Historical background in children with affective disorders. *American Journal of Psychiatry*, 1973, *130*, 1278.

McKnew, D. H., and Cytryn, L. Urinary metabolites in chronically depressed children. *Journal of the American Academy of Child Psychiatry*, 1979, *18*, 608.

McKnew, D. H.; Cytryn, L.; Efron, A. M.; Gershon, E. S.; and Bunney, W. E., Jr. Offspring of manic-depressive patients. *British Journal of Psychiatry*, 1979, *134*, 148.

McKnew, D. H.; Cytryn, L.; and Lamour, M. Fantasy in childhood depression and other forms of psychopathology. *Annals of the American Society for Adolescent Psychiatry*, 1982, 292.

McKnew, D. H.; Cytryn, L.; and Lamour, M. *Disturbances in the Offspring of Manic Depressives*. Paper presented at the Annual Meeting of the American Psychiatric Association, Toronto, May 1982.

McKnew, D. H.; Cytryn, L.; Rapoport, J.; Buchsbaum, M.; Gershon, E.; Lamour, M.; and Hamovit, J. Lithium in children of lithium-responding parents. *Psychiatry Research*, 1981, *4*, 171.

McKnew, D. H.; Cytryn, L.; and White, I. Clinical and biochemical correlates of hypomania in a child: case report. *Journal of the American Academy of Child Psychiatry*, 1974, *13*, 576.

McKnew, D. H.; Cytryn, L.; and Zahn-Waxler, C. *Risk Research in Childhood Depression: Developmental Aspects*. Paper presented at the Annual Meeting of the American Psychological Association, Washington, D. C., August 1982.

Mendlewicz, J., and Gleiss, J. L. Linkage studies with X-hromosome markers in bipolar (manic-depressive) and unipolar (depressive) illness. *Biological Psychiatry*, 1974, *9*, 261.

Mendlewicz, J.; Fleiss, J. L.; Cataldo, M.; and Rainer, J. D. Accuracy of the family history method in affective illness. *Archives of General Psychiatry*, 1975, *32*, 309.

Meyer, A. Construction formulation of schizophrenia. In *The Collected Papers of Adolf Meyer, II*. Baltimore: Johns Hopkins University Press, 1951.

Moebius, P. J. *Diagnostik der Nervenkrankheiten*. Leipzig: V. Vogel, 1894.

Murphy, L. *The Widening World of Childhood*. New York: Basic Books, 1962.

Nissen, G. *Das Depressive Syndrom im Kindes-und Jugenalter*. Berlin: Springer Verlag, 1971.

Noyes, A. P. *Modern Clinical Psychiatry*. Philadelphia: W. B. Saunders, 1948.

Nurnberger, J. I., and Gershon, E. S. Genetics of affective disorders. In E. Paykel (ed.). *Handbook of Affective Disorders*. London: Churchill Livingston, 1982.

Otto, U. Suicidal attempts in childhood and adolescence—a follow-up study. In A. L. Annell (ed.). *Depressive States in Childhood and Adolescence*. Stockholm: Almquist & Wiksell, 1971.

Penot, B. Caracteristiques et devenir des depressions de la deuxieme enfance. In A. L. Annell (ed.). *Depressive States in Childhood and Adolescence*. Stockholm: Almquist & Wiksell, 1971.

Pfeffer, C. R.; Conte, H. R.; Plutchik, R.; and Jerrett, I. Suicidal behavior in latency-age children: an empirical study. *Journal of the American Academy of Child Psychiatry*, 1979, *18*, 679.

Pfeffer, C. R.; Conte, H. R.; Plutchik, R.; and Jerrett, I. Suicidal behavior in latency-age children: an outpatient population. *Journal of the American Academy of Child Psychiatry*, 1980, *19*, 703.

Pfeffer, C. R.; Plutchik, R.; and Mizruchi, M. S. *Suicidal and Assaultive Behavior in Children: Classification, Measurement, and Interrelations*. Paper presented at the Annual Meeting of the American Psychiatric Association in Toronto, May 1982.

Pierson, G. M. *Emotional Disorders of Children*. New York: W. W. Norton, 1949.

Post, R. M.; Kotin, J.; Goodwin, F. K.; and Gordon, E. K. Psychomotor activity and cerebrospinal fluid amine metabolites in affective illness. *American Journal of Psychiatry*, 1973, *130*, 67.

Poznanski, E. O.; Carroll, B. J.; Bamejas, M. C.; Cook, S. C.; and Grossman, J. A. The dexamethasone suppression test in prepubertal depressed children. *American Journal of Psychiatry*, 1982, *139*, 321.

Poznanski, E. O.; Krahenbuhl, V.; and Zrull, J. P. Childhood depression: a longitudinal perspective. *Journal of the American Academy of Child Psychiatry*, 1976, *15*, 491.

Poznanski, E., and Zrull, J. P. Childhood depression. *Archives of General Psychiatry*, 1970, *23*, 8.

Puig-Antich, J.; Blau, S.; Marx, N.; Breengill, L.; and Chambers, S. W. Prepubertal major depressive disorder, a pilot study. *Journal of the American Academy of Child Psychiatry*, 1978, *17*, 695.

Puig-Antich, J.; Chambers, W.; Halpern, I.; Hanlow, C.; and Sachar, E. J. Cortisol hypersecretion in prepubertal major depressive illness: a preliminary report. *Psychoendocrinology*, 1979, *4*, 191.

Puig-Antich, J.; Novacenko, H.; Davies, M.; Chambers, W. J.; Tabrizi, M. A.; Krawiec, V.; Ambrosini, P. J.; and Sachar, E. J. *Growth Hormone Secretion in Prepubertal Major Depressive Children in Response to Insulin-Induced Hypoglycemia*. Paper presented at the Annual Meeting of the American Academy of Child Psychiatry in Washington, D. C., October 1982.

Puig-Antich, J.; Perel, J. M.; Lupatkin, W.; Chamber, W. J.; Shea, C.; Tabrizi, M. A.; and Stiller, R. L. Plasma levels of imipramine and desmethylimipramine and clinical response in prepubertal major depressive disorder: a preliminary report. *Journal of the American Academy of Child Psychiatry*, 1979, *18*, 616.
Rado, S. The problem of melancholia. *International Journal of Psychoanalysis*, 1928, *9*, 420.
Rado, S. Psychodynamics of depression from the etiologic point of view. *Psychosomatic Medicine*, 1951, *13*, 51.
Rapoport, J. L. Psychopharmacology of childhood depression. In D. F. Klein and R. Gittelman-Klein (eds.). *Progress in Psychiatric Drug Treatment, II.* New York: Brunner / Mazel, 1976.
Rapoport, J. L., and Mikkelsen, E. J. Lithium in child and adolescent psychiatry. In J. Werry (ed.). *Pediatric Psychopharmacology.* New York: Brunner / Mazel, 1977.
Rapoport, J. L.; Quinn, P. O.; Bradbard, G.; Riddle, K. D.; and Brooks, E. Imipramine and methylphenidate treatments of hyperactive boys. *Archives of General Psychiatry*, 1974, *30*, 789.
Raskin, A. Depression in children: fact or fallacy. In J. G. Schultenbrandt and A. Raskin (eds.). *Depression in Childhood.* New York: Raven Press, 1977.
Reite, M. Maternal separation in monkey infants: a model of depression. In I. Hanin and E. Usdin (eds.). *Animal Models in Psychiatry.* Oxford: Pergamon Press, 1977.
Remschmidt, H.; Strunk, P.; Methmer, C.; and Tegeler, E. Kinder endogendepressiven eltern. *Fortschritte der Neurologie, Psychiatrie und Ihrer Grenzgebiet*, 1973, *41*, 326.
Rie, H. E. Depression in childhood: a survey of some pertinent contributions. *Journal of the American Academy of Child Psychiatry*, 1966, *5*, 653.
Rochlin, G. The loss complex. *Journal of the American Psychoanalyic Association*, 1959, *7*, 299.
Rosenthal, D. *Genetic Theory and Human Behavior.* New York: McGraw-Hill, 1970.
Rosenthal, P. A., and Rosenthal, S. *Fact or Fallacy of Preschool-Age Suicide.* Paper presented at the Annual Meeting of the American Psychiatric Association, Toronto, May 1982.
Rosenthal, S. H., and Gudeman, J. E. The endogenous depressive pattern. *Archives of General Psychiatry*, 1967, *16*, 241.
Rutter, M. *Children of Sick Parents.* Maudsley Monograph no. 16. London: Oxford University Press, 1966.
Sacher, E. J. Twenty-four-hour cortisol secretory patterns in depressed and manic patients. In W. H. Gispen, T. B. Van Wimersma Greidanus, B. Bohus, and D. deWied (eds.). *Progress in Brain Research.* Amsterdam: Elsevier Press, 1975.
Sandler, J. The background of safety. *International Journal of Psychoanalysis*, 1960, *41*, 352.
Sandler, J.; Holder, A.; and Meers, D. The ego ideal and the ideal self. *Psychoanalytic Study of the Child*, 1963, *18*, 139.
Sandler, J., and Joffe, W. G. Notes on childhood depression. *International Journal of Psychoanalysis*, 1965, *46*, 88.
Schachter, M. The cyclothymic states in the prepubescent child. *Nervous Child*, 1952, *9*, 357.
Schachter, M. Etude des depressions et des episodes depressifs chez l'enfant et l'adolescent. *Acta Paedopsychiatrica*, 1971, *38*, 191.
Schildkraut, J. J. The catecholamine hypothesis of affective disorders—a review of supporting evidence. *American Journal of Psychiatry*, 1965, *122*, 509.

Schildkraut, J. J. Neuropsychopharmacology and the Affective Disorders. Boston: Little, Brown & Co., 1970.

Schildkraut, J. J. Biogenic amine metabolism in depressive illness. In T. A. Williams, M. M. Katz, and J. A. Shield (eds.). Recent Advances of the Psychobiology of the Depressive Illness. Washington: U. S. Government Printing Office, 1972.

Schildkraut, J. J. The catecholamine hypothesis of affective disorders—a review of supporting evidence. The American Journal of Psychiatry, 1965, 50, 122.

Schildkraut, J. J.; Orsulak, P. J.; Geideman, J. E.; Schatzberg, A. F.; Rohde, W. A.; LaBrie, R. A.; Cahill, J. F.; Cole, J. O.; and Frazier, S. H. Recent studies of the role of catecholamines in the pathophysiology and classification of depressive disorders. In E. Usdin, D. A. Hamburg, and J. D. Barchas (eds.). Neuroregulators and Psychiatric Disorders. New York: Oxford University Press, 1977.

Schou, M. Lithium in psychiatric therapy and prophylaxis. In A. L. Annell (ed.). Depressive States in Childhood and Adolescence. Stockholm: Almquist & Wiksell, 1971.

Seiden, R. H. Suicide Among Youth. Washington: U. S. Public Health Service, 1971.

Seligman, M. E. Fall into helplessness. Psychology Today, 1973, 7, 43.

Seligman, M. E., and Peterson, C. A Learned Helplessness Perspective on Childhood Depression: Theory and Research. Paper presented at Social Science Research Council conference on "Depressive Disorders: Developmental Perspective," Philadelphia, April 1982.

Shaffer, D., and Fisher, P. The epidemiology of suicide in children and young adolescents. Journal of the American Academy of Child Psychiatry, 1981, 21, 545.

Shaw, C. R., and Lucas, A. R. Psychoneurosis. In C. R. Shaw and A. R. Lucas (eds.). The Psychiatric Disorders of Childhood. New York: Appleton-Century, 1970.

Shekim, W. O.; Hardin, C.; Kashani, K.; Hodges, K. K.; Cytryn, L.; and McKnew, D. H. Depression in Hyperactive Boys. Paper presented at the Annual Meeting of the American Academy of Child Psychiatry, Chicago 1980.

Shneidman, E. S. Suicide. In A. M. Friedman, H. I. Kaplan, and B. J. Saddock (eds.). Comprehensive Textbook of Psychiatry. Baltimore: Williams & Wilkins, 1975.

Skeels, H. M. A study of the effects of differential stimulation on mentally retarded children: a follow-up report. American Journal of Mental Deficiency, 1941, 46, 340.

Soblen, R., and Saunders, J. C. Monamine-oxidase inhibitor therapy in adolescent psychiatry. Diseases of the Nervous System, 1961, 2, 96.

Soumi, S. J., and Harlow, H. F. Production and alleviation of depressive behaviors in monkeys. In J. Muser and M. E. P. Seligman (eds.). Psychopathology: Experimental Models. San Francisco: W. H. Freeman, 1977.

Spiel, W. Die Endogenen Psychosen des Kinder und Jugendalters. New York: S. Karger, Basel, 1961.

Spiel, W. A. Studien uber den verlauf und die ercheimungsformen der kindlichen und juvenilen manisch depressive psychosis. In A. L. Annell (ed.). Depressive States in Childhood and Adolescence. Stockholm: Almquist & Wiksell, 1972.

Spitz, R. A. Hospitalism: an inquiry into the genesis of psychiatric conditions in early childhood, I. Psychoanalytic Study of the Child, 1945, 1, 53.

Spitz, R. A. Anaclitic depression: an inquiry into the genesis of psychiatric conditions in early childhood, II. Psychoanalytic Study of the Child, 1946, 2, 312.

Spitzer, L., Endicott, J., and Robins, E. Research diagnostic criteria. Archives of General Psychiatry, 1972, 35, 773.

Strachey, J. The nature of the therapeutic action of psychoanalysis. *International Journal of Psychoanalysis*, 1934, *15*, 127.

Stutte, H. Kinderpsychiatrie und jugendpsychiatrie. In H. W. Gruhle, R. Jung, W. Mayer-Gross, and M. Miller (eds.). *Psychiatrie der Gegenwart*. Berlin: Springer Verlag, 1960.

Stutte, H. Psychosen des kindesalters. In H. Opitz and F. Schmid (eds.). *Handbuch der Kinderheilkunde*. Berlin: Springer Verlag, 1969.

Sweeney, D. R.; Maas, J. W.; and Heninger, G. R. State anxiety, physical activity and urinary 3-methoxy-4-hydroxyphenylethylene glycol excretion. *Archives of General Psychiatry*, 1978, *35*, 1418.

Toolan, J. M. Depression in children and adolescents. *American Journal of Orthopsychiatry*, 1962, *32*, 404.

Toolan, J. M. Suicide in childhood and adolescence. In H. L. P. Resnick (ed.). *Suicidal Behaviors: Diagnosis and Management*. Boston: Little, Brown & Co., 1968.

Van Krevelen, D. A. Zyklothymien in kindesalter. *Acta Paedopsychiatrica*, 1961, *38*, 202.

Van Krevelen, A. A. La mania fantastique des enfants. *Revue de Neuropsychiatric Infantile et d'Hygiene Mentale de l'Enfance*, 1962, *10*, 133.

Weinberg, W. A., and Brumback R. H. Mania in childhood. *Archives of American Journal of Diseases of Children*, 1976, *130*, 380.

Weinberg, W. A.; Rutman, J.; Sullivan, L; Penick, E. C.; and Dietz, S. G. Depression in children referred to an educational diagnostic center: diagnosis and treatment. *Journal of Pediatrics*, 1973, *83*, 1065.

Winnicott, D. W. Hate in the countertransference. *Journal of Psychoanalysis*, 1949, *30*, 69.

Winokur, G. Depression spectrum disease: description and family study. *Comparative Psychiatry*, 1972, *13*, 3.

Winokur, G. Heredity in the affective disorders. In E. J. Anthony and T. Benedek (eds.). *Depression and Human Existence*. Boston: Little, Brown & Co., 1975.

Index